Irish Local Names Explained

BY

P. W. JOYCE, LL.D., M.R.I.A.

ⅭⱤⰰⰾⰾⰰⰿ ⱅⰹⰿⱌⰵⰰⰾⰾ ⱀⰰ Ⱂⱁⰳⰾⰰ

ROBERTS BOOKS

First published 1923
This edition published 1996
ROBERTS WHOLESALE BOOKS LTD
Unit 12
Benson Street Enterprise Centre
Hanover Quay
Dublin 2 Ireland
Tel: 353-1-6777142
Fax: 353-1-6777213

PREFACE

This little volume is a key that will help to open many locks.

It contains a vocabulary of the root words from which Irish place names are most generally formed. It also contains a considerable selection of those names that are best known through the country, and which best exemplify the use of the root words.

By the aid of the roots and examples it will be easy to discover the proper forms and meanings of hundreds of place names not mentioned in the following pages.

Now that an active interest is being taken in the native and correct forms of our place names, this little book cannot fail to be of practical use.

Should more exhaustive information on the subject be desired, it will be found in *The Origin and History of Irish Names of Places* by the same author.

IRISH LOCAL NAMES EXPLAINED.

———◆———

THE PROCESS OF ANGLICISING.

1. SYSTEMATIC CHANGES.

Irish pronunciation preserved.—In anglicising Irish names, the leading general rule is, that the present forms are derived from the ancient Irish, as they were spoken, not as they were written. Those who first committed them to writing, aimed at preserving the original pronunciation, by representing it as nearly as they were able in English letters.

Generally speaking, this principle explains the alterations that were made in the spelling of names, in the process of reducing them from ancient to modern forms; and allowing for the difficulty of representing Irish words by English letters, it will be found that, on the whole, the ancient pronunciation is fairly preserved.

Aspiration.—The most common causes of change in the reduction of Irish names, are aspiration and eclipsis. Some of the Irish consonants are, in certain situations, subject to what is called aspiration; it is indicated by the letter *h*, and it always changes the sound of the consonants.

B and *m* aspirated (*bh*, *mh*) are both sounded like *v* or *w*, and, consequently, where we find *bh* or *mh* in an Irish name, we generally have *v* or *w* in the English form: examples, Ardvally in Donegal and Sligo, in Irish *Ard-bhaile*, high town; Ballinwully in Roscommon, *Baile-an-mhullaigh*, the town of the summit (*mullach*). Sometimes they are represented by *f* in English, as in Boherduff, *Bothar-dubh*, black road : and often they are suppressed, especially in the end of words, or between two vowels, as in Knockdoo, *Cnoc-dubh*, black hill, the same as Knockduff in other places.

For *c* aspirated see page 4.

D and *g* aspirated (*dh, gh*), have a faint guttural sound, not existing in English, and they are conse-quently generally unrepresented in anglicised names; as in Lisnalee, *Lios-na-laegh*, the fort of the calves.

F aspirated (*fh*) totally loses its sound in Irish, and of course is omitted in English; as in Knockanree in Wicklow, *Cnoc-an-fhraeigh*, the hill of the heath.

P aspirated is represented by *f;* as in Ballinfoyle, *Baile-an-phoill*, the town of the hole, the same as Bal-linphuill and Ballinphull elsewhere.

S and *t* aspirated (*sh, th*) both sound the same as English *h;* as in Drumhillagh in Cavan and Monaghan, *Druim-shaileach*, the ridge of the sallows, the same name as Drumsillagh in other counties, in which the original *s* sound is retained.

Eclipsis.—An eclipsed consonant has its sound alto-gether suppressed, the sound of another consonant which is prefixed, being heard instead. Thus when *d* is eclipsed by *n*, it is written *n-d*, but the *n* alone is pronounced. The eclipsed letter is of course always omitted in English.

When a noun is used in the genitive plural, with the article prefixed, its initial consonant is eclipsed. Each consonant has a special eclipsing letter of its own.

B is eclipsed by *m;* Knocknamoe, the name of a place in Queen's County, represents the Irish *Cnoc-na-mbo*, the hill of the cows.

C is eclipsed by *g;* as in Cloonnagashel near Ballin-robe, which ought to have been anglicised Coolnagashel, for the Four Masters write the name *Cuil-na-gcaiseal*, the corner of the *cashels* or stone forts.

D and *g* are both eclipsed by *n;* as in Mullananallog in Monaghan, *Mullach-na-ndealg*, the summit of the thorns or thorn bushes.

F is eclipsed by *bh*, which is represented by *v* in

English; as in Carriguavar in Cork, which is in Irish *Carraig-na-bhfear*, the rock of the men.

P is eclipsed by *b;* as in Gortnaboul in Kerry and Clare, *Gort-na-bpoll*, the field of the holes.

S is eclipsed by *t*, in the genitive singular with the article; as in Ballintaggart, *Baile-an tsagairt*, the town of the priest.

T is eclipsed by *d;* as in Lisnadurk in Fermanagh *Lios-na-dtorc*, the fort of the boars.

2. CORRUPTIONS.

While the majority of names have been modernized in accordance with the principle of preserving the pronunciation, great numbers on the other hand have been contracted and corrupted in a variety of ways. Some of these corruptions took place in the Irish language; but far the greatest number were introduced by the English-speaking people in transferring the words from the Irish to the English language. The following are some of the principal corruptions.

Interchange of l, m, n, r. The interchange of these letters is common in Irish and English, as well as in other languages. We find *l* very often substituted for *r;* as in Shrule, Shruel, Struell, Sroohill, in all of which the final consonant sound should be that of *r*, for they are derived from *Sruthair* [sruher], a stream.

N is sometimes, but not often, changed to *l*, as in Castleconnell near Limerick, which is the castle of the O'Connings, not of the O'Connells, as the present form of the name would indicate.

The change of *n* to *r* is of frequent occurrence, as in Kilmacrenan in Donegal, which should have been called Kilmacnenan, for the Irish authorities write it *Cill-mac-nEnain*, which Colgan translates the church of the sons of Enan, who were contemporaries and relatives of St. Columba.

The change of *l* to *r* is not very common, but we find it in Ballysakeery in Mayo, which is written by Mac-Firbis, *Baile-easa-caoile* [Ballysakeely], the town of the narrow cataract.

M and *n* are occasionally interchanged. For example, the barony of Glenquin in Limerick, should have been called Glenquim, for the Irish is *Gleann-a'-chuim*, the glen of the *cum* or hollow. Kilmainham near Dublin is called Kilmannan by Boate, which is more correct than the present form. The name signifies the church of St. Mainen (Irish *Maighnenn*), who was bishop and abbot there in the seventh century.

Change of ch *and* th, *to* f. The guttural sound of *c* aspirated (*ch*) does not exist in English, and in anglicised names it is occasionally changed to *f;* for example, Knocktopher in Kilkenny, is from the Irish *Cnoc-a'-tochair*, the hill of the *togher* or causeway. *F* is also sometimes substituted for *th;* thus, Tiscoffin in Kilkenny took its name from an old church called *Tigh-scoithin* [Tee-Scoheen], the house of St. Scoithin, who erected his primitive church here towards the close of the sixth century.

Substitution of g *for* d. *D* aspirated is often changed to *g;* as in Drumgonnelly in Louth, which should have been anglicised Drumdonnelly, for the Irish is *Druim-Dhonghaile*, the ridge or long hill of the Donnellys.

Addition of d *after* n; *and of* b *after* m. The letter *d* is often corruptly placed after *n;*—as we find in case of Rathfryland in Down, which is called in Irish *Rath-Fraeileann*, Freelan's fort. *B* is also often placed after *m;* as in Cumber or Comber, the names of several places in the northern counties; the Irish word is *Comar*, which signifies the confluence of two waters, and it is correctly anglicised Cummer and Comer in many other names.

IRISH LOCAL NAMES EXPLAINED.

The following abbreviations have been used in quoting authorities for the
Irish forms:—

"F. M.," The Annals of the Four Masters.
"Book of R.," The Book of Rights (*Leabhar-na-gCeart*).
"Hy F.," The Tribes and Customs of Hy Fiachrach.
"O'Dugan," The topographical Poems of O'Dugan and O'Heeren.
"O'C. Cal.," O'Clery's Calendar of Irish Saints, or, The Martyrology of
Donegal.
"Wars of GG.," The Wars of the *Gaedhil* with the *Gaill* (of the Irish with
the Danes).
"Mart. Tam..," The Martyrology of Tallaght.

The Irish forms are always in Italics. The Irish root words are fully explained in the Vocabulary at the end of the book.
The pronunciation of the principal Irish words is given in brackets, as
nearly as can be represented by English letters.

Abbeyfeale in Limerick; *Mainistir-na-Feile*, the monastery or abbey of the river Feale.

Abbeygormican in Galway; the abbey of the O'Cor-
macans.

Abbeylara or Lara in Longford, *Leath-rath*, F. M.
[Lah-rah], half rath or fort.

Abbeyleix; the abbey of the old principality of Leix,
so called from a monastery founded there in 1183 by
Conor O'Moore. In the reign of Felimy the Lawgiver (A. D. 111 to 119), this territory was given by
the king of Leinster to *Lughaidh Laeighseach* [Lewy
Leeshagh], Conall Carnach's grandson, for helping
to expel the Munstermen who had seized on Ossory.
Lewy's descendants, the O'Moores, took from him
the tribe name, *Laeighis* [Leesh], and their territory
was called by the same name, now modernized to
Leix.

Abbeyshrule in Longford; from a monastery founded
there by one of the O'Farrells. It was anciently
called *Sruthair* [Sruher], F. M., i. e. the stream, of
which Shrule is a corruption.

Abbeystrowry in Cork; the same name as the last.
The *sruthair* or stream from which it was called,
gave name also to Bealnashrura (the *beal* or ford-
mouth of the stream) a village situated at an ancient
ford.

Achonry in Sligo, *Achadh-Chonaire* [Aha-Conary], F. M., Conary's field.

Adare in Limerick; *Ath-dara* [Ah-dara], F. M., the ford of the oak tree. A large oak must have anciently overshadowed the old ford on the Maigue.

Addergoole, Addragool, Adrigole, Adrigoole; *Eadar-dha-ghabhal* [Adragoul], i. e. (a place) between two (river) forks.

Aderrig; *Ath-dearg*, red ford. See Aghaderg.

Affane on the Blackwater below Cappoquin; *Ath-mheadhon*, [Ah-vane], F. M., middle ford.

Agha in several counties; *Achadh* [Aha], a field.

Aghaboe in Queen's County, where St. Canice of Kilkenny had his principal church. Adamnan in his Life of St. Columkille, written in the seventh century, has the following passage, which settles the meaning:—" St. Canice being in the monastery which is called in Latin *Campulus bovis* (i. e. the field of the cow), but in Irish *Ached-bou.*"

Aghaboy; *Achadh-buidhe* [Aha-boy], yellow field.

Aghacross near Kildorrery in Cork; the ford of the cross; probably from a cross erected in connexion with St. Molaga's adjacent establishment, to mark a ford on the Funcheon. See Templemolaga.

Aghada near Cork; *Ath-fhada* [Ahada], long ford.

Aghaderg; *Ath-dearg*, red ford. See Aderrig.

Aghadoe near Killarney; *Achadh-dá-eó* [Aha-daw-o], F. M., the field of the two yew trees.

Aghadowey in Derry; *Achadh-Dubhthaigh* [Ahaduffy], O'C. Cal., Duffy's field.

Aghadown and **Aghadoon;** the field of the *dun* or fort

Aghadreen, Aghadreenagh, Aghadreenan, Aghadrinagh; the field of the *dreens* or sloe bushes (*draeighean*).

Aghafad, Aghafadda; long field.

Aghagallon; the field of the *gallan* or standing stone.

Aghagower in Mayo; the correct name would be Aghafower, for the ancient form, as found in the old Lives of St. Patrick, is *Achadh-fobhair*, the field of the spring, from a celebrated well, now called St. Patrick's well. The present form is written in Hy F., *Achadh-gabhair*, which means the field of the goat.

Aghamore; *Achadh-mór*, great field.

Aghanloo; *Athan-Lugha*, Lugh's or Lewy's little ford.

Aghavea in Fermanagh; *Achaah-beithe* [Ahabehy], F. M., the field of the birch trees.

Aghaveagh in Donegal and Tyrone; same as last.

Aghavilla, Aghaville, Aghavilly; *Achadh-bhile*, the field of the *bilĕ* or old tree.

Aghaviller in Kilkenny; *Achadh-biorair* [Ahabirrer], F. M., the field of the watercresses (*r* changed to *l*).

Aghindarragh in Tyrone; the field of the oak.

Aghintamy near Monaghan; *Achadh-an-tsamhaidh*, the field of the sorrel.

Aghmacart in Queen's County; the field of Art's son.

Aghnamullen in Monaghan; the field of the mills.

Aghnaskea, Aghnaskeagh, Aghnaskew; *Achadh-na-sceach*, the field of the white-thorn bushes.

Aghowle in Wicklow; *Achadh-abhla*, the field of the apple trees.

Aglish; *Eaglais* [aglish], a church.

Aglishcloghane in Tipperary; the church of the *clogh-aun* or row of stepping stones.

Aglishcormick in Limerick; St. Cormac's church.

Aglishdrinagh in Cork; *Eaglais-draeighneach*, the church of the *dreens* or sloe bushes.

Agolagh in Antrim; *Ath-gobhlach*, forked ford.

Ahane, Ahaun; *Athán*, little ford.

Ahaphuca; the ford of the *pooka* or spright.

Ahascragh in Galway; *Ath-eascrach*, F. M., the ford of the *esker* or sand-hill.

Aille; *Aill*, a cliff.

Alleen; *Aillin*, a little cliff.

Alt; *Alt*, a height, the side of a glen.

Altan; little cliff or glen side.

Altaturk; the glen side of the boar (*torc*).

Altavilla; the glen side of the *bilĕ* or old tree.

Altinure; *Alt-an-iubhair* [yure], the glen side of the yew tree.

Altnaveagh and Altnaveigh; *Alt-na-bhfiach*, the cliff or glen side of the *fiachs* or ravens.

Anna; same as Annagh, which see.

Annabella near Mallow; *Eanach-bilĕ*, the marsh of the *bilĕ* or old tree.

Annaclone; the marsh of the meadow (*cluain*).

Annacotty near Limerick; *Atḣ-na-coite*, the ford of the *cot* or little boat.

Annacramph in Armagh and Monaghan; *Eanach-creamha*, the marsh of the wild garlick.

Annaduff; *Eanach-dubh*, F. M., black marsh.

Annagh; *Eanach*, a marsh.

Annaghaskin in Dublin, near Bray; *Eanach-easgann*, the marsh of the eels.

Annaghbeg, Annaghmore; little marsh, great marsh.

Annahagh, Annahaia in Monaghan and Armagh; *Ath-na-haithe*, the ford of the kiln (*aith*).

Annahavil; *Eanach-abhaill*, the marsh of the orchard (*abhall*).

Annahilt in Down; *Eanach-eilte*, the marsh of the doe (*eilit*).

Annakisha; the ford of the *kish* or wickerwork causeway.

Annalong in Down; *Ath-na-long*, the ford of the ships (*long*): the ford was near the place where vessels used to be moored or anchored.

Annamoe in Wicklow; *Ath-na-mbo*, the ford of the cows (*bo*).

Anny; same as Annagh, which see.

Arboe in Tyrone; *Ard-bo*, the cow's height.

Ard; high; a height.

Ardagh; *Ard-achadh* [Ard-aha], high field.

Ardaghy; same as Ardagh.

Ardan, Ardane, Ardaun; little *ard* or height.

Ardara in Donegal; *Ard-a'-raith*, the height of the rath, from a hill near the village, on which stands a conspicuous fort.

Ardataggle, Ardateggle; *Ard-a'-tseagail*, the height of the rye (*seagal*).

Ardbane, Ardbaun; white height.

Ardbeg; little height.

Ardbraccan in Meath; St. Brecan's height. St. Brecan erected a church here in the sixth century, some

time previous to his removal to the great island of
Aran, where he had his chief establishment.

Ardcarn ; the height of the *carn* or monumental heap.

Ardcath; the height of the battle (*cath*).

Ardee in Louth. Old English form Atherdee, which
represents the Irish *Ath-Fhirdia* [Ahirdee], as it is
written in Irish authorities, the ford of Ferdia, a
chieftain who was slain there in battle by Cuchullin
in the first century.

Ardeen in Cork and Kerry; little height.

Ardeevin; *Ard-aeibhinn*, beautiful height.

Arderin; the height of Erin or Ireland.

Ardfert in Kerry; *Ard-ferta*, F. M., the height of the
grave. Sometimes called Ardfert-Brendan, from St.
Brendan the navigator, who founded a monastery
there in the sixth century.

Ardfinnan in Tipperary; the height of St. Finan, who
founded a monastery there in the seventh century.

Ardgeeha; *Ard-gaeithe*, height of the wind.

Ardglass; *Ard-glas*, green height.

Ardgoul; *Ard-gabhal*, high fork.

Ardkeen; *Ardcaein*, beautiful height.

Ardkill; high church or wood (*cill* or *coill*).

Ardlougher; *Ard-luachra*, rushy height.

Ardmayle ; *Ard-Maille*, F. M., Malley's height.

Ardmeen ; smooth height.

Ardmore in various counties; great height.

Ardmulchan in Meath; *Ard-Maelchon*, F. M., Mael
chon's height.

Ardnacrusha, Ardnacrushy; the height of the cross.

Ardnageeha, Ardnageehy; the height of the wind
(*gaeth*).

Ardnanean; the height of the birds (*en*).

Ardnapreaghaun ; the height of the *prehauns* or crows.

Ardnarea near Ballina; *Ard-na-riaghadh* [reea], Hy F.,
the hill of the executions. Four persons were exe-
cuted here in the seventh century, for the murder of
Kellach, bishop of Kilmore-Moy.

Ardnurcher in Westmeath ; a corruption of Athnurcher,
from *Ath-an-urchair*, F. M., the ford of the cast or
throw. According to a very ancient legend, a battle

was fought here in the first century, between the Connaught and Ulster forces. Keth Mac Magach, a Connaught chief, threw a hard round ball at Conor mac Nessa, king of Ulster, and struck him on the head, from the effects of which the king died seven years afterwards.

Ardpatrick; St. Patrick's height.

Ardrahan; *Ard-rathain,* the height of the ferns.

Ardskeagh; the height of the *skeaghs* or bushes.

Ardstraw in Tyrone; *Ard-sratha* [Ard-srawha], F. M., the height of (or near) the river holm.

Ardvally in Donegal and Sligo.　See page 1.

Ardvarna, Ardvarness, Ardvarney, Ardvarnish; *Ard-bhearna* and *Ard-bhearnas,* high gap.

Arless in Queen's County; *Ard-lios,* high fort.

Armagh; written in all Irish authorities *Ard-Macha,* which, in the Book of Armagh, is translated *Altitudo Machæ,* Macha's height.　From Queen Macha of the golden hair, who founded the palace of Emania, 300 years B. C.

Armoy in Antrim; *Airthir-Maighe* [Arhir-moy], F. M., eastern plain.

Artimacormack in Antrim; *Ard-tighe-Mic-Cormaic,* the height of Mac Cormack's house.

Artrea in Derry; *Ard-Trea* (Mart. Taml.), Trea's height.　The virgin St. Trea flourished in the fifth century.

Askeaton; took its name from the cataract on the Deel near the town, which the F. M. call *Eas-Gephtine* [Ass-Geftinĕ], Gephtine's cataract.

Assan, Assaun; small *ass* or waterfall.

Assaroe at Ballyshannon.　The Book of Leinster states that *Aedh-Ruadh* [Ay-roo], queen Macha's father (see Armagh), was drowned in this cataract, which was thence called from him *Eas-Aedha-Ruaidh* [Assayroo], *Aedh-Ruadh's* waterfall.

Assey on the Boyne in Meath.　The F. M. record that in A. D. 524 " the battle of *Ath-Sithe* [Ah-Shee] was gained by *Muircheartach* (king of Ireland) against the Leinstermen, where *Sithe* [Shee] the son of *Dian* was slain, from whom *Ath-Sithe* (*Sithe's* ford) is called."

Athenry; *Ath-na-riogh* [ree], F. M., the ford of the kings.

Athgoe in Dublin ; the ford of the *gow* or smith.

Athlacca in Limerick; from a ford on the Morning Star river, called *Ath-leacach*, stony ford.

Athleague in Roscommon; *Ath-liag,* F. M., the ford of the stones.

Athlone ; from the ancient ford over the Shannon, called in Irish authorities *Ath-Luain*, the ford of *Luan*, a man's name.

Athneasy in Limerick; called in the F. M., *Ath-na-nDeise* [Athnaneasy], the ford of (the tribe of) the *Desii*, who inhabited the old territory of *Deisbeag*, round Knockany.

Athnid in Tipperary; the ford of the *nead* or bird's nest.

Athnowen, a parish near Ballincollig in Cork; from a ford on the river Bride, called *Ath-'n-uamhainn* [Ath-nooan], the ford of the cave (*uaimh*), from the great limestone cave at "The Ovens," near the ford.

Athy. One of the battles between Lewy and the Munstermen (see Abbeyleix), was fought at a ford on the Barrow, where a Munster chief, *Ae*, was slain; and from him the place was called *Ath-I* (Wars of GG), the ford of *Ae*.

Attavally; *Ait-a'-bhaile*, the site of the *bally* or town.

Atti or Atty in the beginning of a name, is the anglicised form of *áit-tighe* [aut-tee], the place or site of a house (*ait* and *teach*).

Attidermot; the site of Dermot's house.

Attiduff; the site of the black house.

Attykit; the site of *Ceat's* or Keth's house.

Aughall in Tipperary and Aughil in Derry; *Eochaill*, the yew wood (*eo* and *coill*). See Youghal and Oghill.

Aughinish; *Each-inis*, F. M., the island of horses.

Aughnacloy; *Achadh-na-cloiche* [Ahanacloha], the field of the stone.

Aughnahoy; *Achadh-na-haithe*, the field of the kiln (*aith*).

Aughnanure near Oughterard in Galway; *Achadh-na-*

niúbhar [Ahananure], the field of the yew trees.
One of the old yews still remains.

Aughnish ; same as Aughinish.

Aughrim; the name is written in Irish documents,
Each-dhruim [Agh-rim : *dh* silent], which Colgan
translates *Equi-mons*, the hill, *druim*, or ridge, of the
horse (*each*).

Aughris, Aughrus ; *Each-ros*, F. M., the peninsula of
the horses.

Avalbane, Avalreagh ; white orchard, grey orchard
(*abhall*).

Avonmore, Avonbeg ; great river, little river (*abhainn*).

Aubeg ; *Abh-bheag*, little river.

Ayle ; same as Aille, which see.

Bahana ; same as Behanagh, which see.

Bailey lighthouse at Howth ; from the old *bally* or for
tress of Criffan, king of Ireland in the first century,
on the site of which it was built.

Balbriggan in Dublin ; *Baile-Breacain*, Brecan's town.

Baldoyle·in Dublin ; *Baile-Dubhghoill*, *Dubhghall's* or
Doyle's town.

Balfeddock ; the town of the *feadogs* or plovers.

Balgeeth in Meath ; the town of the wind (*gaeth*).

Balla in Mayo.   In the Life of St. Mochua, we are told
that before the saint founded his monastery there in
the seventh century, the place was called *Ros-dairbh-
reach* [Ros-dar´áragh], i. e. oak grove ; that he enclosed the wells of his establishment with a *balla* or
wall ; and that hence the place received the new name
of Balla.

Ballagh ; *Bealach*, a road or pass.

Ballaghaderreen in Mayo ; the road of the *derreen* or
little oak wood.

Ballaghbehy ; the road of the birch (*beith*).

Ballaghboy ; yellow road (*buidhe*).

Ballaghkeen in Wexford ; beautiful road (*caein*).

Ballaghkeeran ; the road of the *keerans* or quicken trees.

Ballaghmore ; great road.

Ballard ; *Baile-ard*, high town.

Ballee in Down ; written in the Taxation of 1306,

Baliath; from the Irish *Baile-atha,* the town of the ford.

Balleen; little *bally* or town.

Ballina, the name of many places; *Bel-an-atha* [Bellanaha], the mouth of the ford.

Ballinabarny; the town of the *bearna* or gap.

Ballinaboy in Cork, Galway, and Roscommon; *Bel-an-atha-buidhe,* the mouth of the yellow ford.

Ballinaclogh; the town of the stones (*cloch*).

Ballinacor, Ballinacur, Ballinacurra; *Baile-na-corra,* the town of the weir.

Ballinafad; *Bel-an-atha-fada* [Bellanafadda], the mouth of the long ford.

Ballinagar; *Bel-atha-na-gcarr* [Bellanagar], the ford-mouth of the cars.

Ballinahinch; the town of the *inis* or island.

Ballinakill; the town of the church or wood.

Ballinalack in Westmeath; *Bel-atha-na-leac* [Bellanalack], the mouth of the ford of the flag-stones.

Ballinalee and Ballinalea; *Bel-atha-na-laegh,* the ford-mouth of the calves.

Ballinamona; *Baile-na-mona,* the town of the bog.

Ballinamore; *Bel-an-atha-moir,* the mouth of the great ford.

Ballinamought near Cork; *Baile-na-mbocht,* the town of the poor people (*bocht*).

Ballinard; the town of the *ard* or height.

Ballinascarty; the town of the *scart* or thicket.

Ballinasloe; *Bel-atha-na-sluaigheadh* [Bellanaslooa], F. M., the ford-mouth of the hosts or gatherings.

Ballinaspick, Ballinaspig; *Baile-an-easpuig,* the town of the bishop.

Ballinastraw; the town of the *srath* or river-holm.

Ballinchalla on Lough Mask in Mayo; *Baile-an-chala,* the town of the *callow* or landing place.

Ballinclare; the town of the *clar* or plain.

Ballincloghan; the same as Ballycloghan.

Ballincollig; *Baile-an-chullaigh,* the town of the boar.

Ballincurra, Ballincurrig, Ballincurry; *Baile-an-churraigh,* the town of the *currach* or marsh.

Ballinderry; the town of the *derry* or oak wood.

Ballindrait, Ballindrehid ; *Baile-an-droichid,* the town of the bridge.

Ballineddan in Wicklow ; *Baile-an-fheadáin,* the town of the *feadan* or streamlet.

Ballinfoyle in Galway and Wicklow ; see page 2.

Ballingaddy ; the town of the thief (*gadaighe*), i. e. the black thief O'Dwane.

Ballingarrane ; the town of the *garran* or shrubbery.

Ballingarry ; *Baile-an-gharrdha,* the town of the garden.

Ballinglanna, Ballinglen ; the town of the glen.

Ballingowan ; the town of the smith (*gobha*).

Ballinlass, Ballinlassa, Ballinlassy, Ballinliss ; the town of the *lios* or fort.

Ballinlough ; the town of the lake.

Ballinloughan, Ballinloughaun ; the town of the little lake.

Ballinlug, Ballinluig ; the town of the *lug* or hollow.

Ballinphuill, Ballinphull ; see page 2.

Ballinree ; sometimes *Baile-an-fhraeigh,* the town of the heath (*fraech*) ; sometimes *Baile-an-righ,* the town of the king.

Ballinrobe ; the town of the river Robe.

Ballinrostig ; Roche's town.

Ballinspittle ; the town of the *spital* or hospital.

Ballintaggart ; see page 3.

Ballinteer ; *Baile-an-tsaeir,* the town of the carpenter.

Ballintemple ; the town of the *temple* or church.

Ballinteskin ; *Baile-an-tsescenn,* the town of the morass.

Ballintlea, Ballintleva, Ballintlevy, Ballintlieve ; *Baile-an-tsleibhe,* the town of the mountain (*sliabh*).

Ballintober ; the town of the well.

Ballintogher ; the town of the *togher* or causeway.

Ballintubbert, Ballintubbrid ; same as Ballintober.

Ballinure ; the town of the yew tree (*iubhar*).

Ballinvally ; *Baile-an-bhealaigh,* the town of the road.

Ballinvarrig, Ballinvarry ; Barry's town.

Ballinvella, Ballinvilla ; *Baile-an-bhile,* the town of the *bilĕ* or ancient tree.

Ballinvoher ; *Baile-an-bhothair,* the town of the road.

Ballinvreena in Limerick and Tipperary ; the town of the *bruighean* [breen] or fairy mansion.

Ballinwillin; *Baile-an-mhuilinn,* ·the town of the mill.

Ballinwully in Roscommon; see page 1.

Ballytore in Kildare took its name from a ford on the river Greece; *Bel-atha-a'-tuair* [Bellatoor], the ford mouth of the *tuar* or bleach green.

Ballyard; high town.

Ballybaan, Ballybane, Ballybaun; white town.

Ballybay in Monaghan; *Bel-atha-beithe* [Bellabehy], the ford mouth of the birch.

Ballybeg; small town.

Ballyboe; i. e. "cow-land," a measure of land.

Ballybofey in Donegal. The correct old name is *Srath-bofey.* Some occupier named *Fiach* or Fay must have in past times kept his cows on the holm along the Finn; *Srath-bo-Fiaich*, F.M., the river holm of Fiach's cows.

Ballyboghil in county Dublin; the town of the *bachal* or crozier; from St. Patrick's crozier.

Ballyboley; the town of the *booley* or dairy place.

Ballybough near Dublin; *Baile-bocht*, poor town; the same as Ballybought in other places.

Ballyboy in King's County; written in Irish authorities *Baile-atha-buidhe* [Ballyaboy], the town of the yellow ford; the name is common in other counties and sometimes means yellow town (*Baile-buidhe*)

Ballybrack; speckled town.

Ballybrannagh; Walsh's town. The proper name Walsh is in Irish *Breathnach* [Branagh], i. e. Briton.

Ballybunnion in Kerry; Bunnion's town.

Ballycahan, Ballycahane; O'Cahan's town.

Ballycahill; Cahill's or O'Cahill's town.

Ballycastle in Antrim; the town of the castle.

Ballycastle in Mayo; the town of the *cashel* or circular stone fort.

Ballyclare; the same as Ballinclare.

Ballyclerahan in Tipperary; O'Clerahan's town.

Ballyclogh, Ballyclohy; the town of the stones.

Ballycloghan; the town of the *cloghan* or row of stepping stones across a river.

Ballyclug in Antrim; the town of the bell ·*log*).

Ballycolla; the town of Colla, a man's nam

Ballyconnell in Cavan. According to tradition, Conall Carnagh, one of the most renowned of the Red Branch knights of Ulster, was slain here in the first century; hence it was called *Bel-atha-Chonaill*, the mouth of the ford of Conall.

Ballycormick; Cormac's or O'Cormac's town.

Ballycullane; O'Cullane's or O'Collins's town.

Ballydehob in Cork; *Bel-atha-da-chab*, the ford of the two *cabs* or mouths; from some local feature.

Ballyduff; black town.

Ballyea; O'Hea's or Hayes's town.

Ballyeighter; *Baile-iochtar*, lower town.

Ballyfoyle; the town of the hole (*poll*).

Ballygarran, Ballygarraun; the town of the *garran* or shrubbery.

Ballyglass; green town.

Ballygowan; the town of the smith (*gobha*).

Ballyheige in Kerry; *Baile-ui-Thadg*, the town of O'Teige.

Ballyhooly near Mallow; took its name from an ancient ford on the Blackwater, called in the Book of Lismore *Ath-ubhla* [Ahoola]; the ford of the apples. The people now call it in Irish *Baile-atha-ubhla* (which they pronounce *Blaa-hoola*), the town of the apple ford, which has been shortened to the present name.

Ballykeel; *Baile-cael*, narrow town.

Ballyknock; the town of the hill.

Ballyknockan, Ballyknockane; the town of the little hill.

Ballylanders in Limerick; Landers's town, from an English family of that name.

Ballylig; the town of the *lug* or hollow.

Ballylongford in Kerry; *Bel-atha-longphuirt*, the ford-mouth of the *longphort* or fortress; because it led to Carrigafoyle castle, two miles off.

Ballylough, Ballyloughan, Ballyloughaun; the town of the lake.

Ballylusk, Ballylusky; *Baile-loisgthe*, burnt town; from the practice of burning the surface in tillage.

Ballymena, Ballymenagh ; *Baile-meadhonach*, middle town.

Ballymoney ; the town of the shrubbery (*muine*).

Ballymore ; great town; sometimes when the place is on a river it is *Bel-atha-moir* [Bellamore], the mouth of the great ford.

Ballymote ; *Baile-an-mhota*, F. M., the town of the moat or mound.

Ballynabarna, Ballynabarny, Ballynabearna ; the town of the gap. See Ballinabarny.

Ballynaboley, Ballynaboola, Ballynabooley ; the town of the *booley* or dairy place (*buaile*). See Ballyboley.

Ballynacally ; the town of the *calliagh* or hag.

Ballynacarrick, Ballynacarrig, Ballynacarriga, Ballynacarrigy ; the town of the rock (*carraig*).

Ballynaclogh, Ballynacloghy ; *Baile-na-cloiche*, the town of the *cloch* or stone.

Ballynacor, Ballynacorra ; the town of the weir (*cora*).

Ballynacourty ; the town of the *court* or mansion.

Ballynagall, Ballynagaul ; the town of the *Galls* or foreigners.

Ballynagard ; the town of the *ceards* or artificers.

Ballynagee, Ballynageeha ; town of the wind (*gaeth*).

Ballynageeragh ; the town of the sheep (*caera*).

Ballynaglogh ; *Baile-na-gcloch*, the town of the stones.

Ballynagore ; the town of the goats (*gabhar*).

Ballynagowan ; the town of the smiths (*gobha*).

Ballynagran ; *Baile-na-gcrann*, the town of the trees.

Ballynahaglish ; the town of the church (*eaglais*).

Ballynahinch ; the town of the *inis* or island.

Ballynahone, Ballynahown, Ballynahowna ; the town of the river (*abhainn*).

Ballynahow ; the town of the river (*abh*).

Ballynakill, Ballynakilla, Ballynakilly ; the town of the church or wood (*cill* or *coill*).

Ballynalacken ; the town of the *leacan* or hill side.

Ballynamona ; the town of the bog (*móin*).

Ballynamuck ; the town of the pigs (*muc*).

Ballynamuddagh ; *Baile-na-mbodach*, the town of the *bodachs* or churls.

Ballynaraha; the town of the rath or fort.

Ballynatona, Ballynatone; the town of the *backside* or hill (*tóin*).

Ballynatray; the town of the strand (*traigh*).

Ballyneety; *Baile-an-Fhaeite*, the town of White, a family name of English origin.

Ballyness; the town of the waterfall (*eas*).

Ballynew, Ballynoe; *Baile-nua*, new town.

Ballynure; *Baile-an-iubhair*, the town of the yew.

Ballyorgan in Limerick; Organ's or Horgan's town.

Ballyragget in Kilkenny; *Bel-atha-Raghat*, F. M., Ragat's ford-mouth.

Ballyroe; *Baile-ruadh*, red town.

Ballyroosky; the town of the *rusk* or marsh.

Ballysadare in Sligo; originally *Eas-dara* [Assdara], the cataract of the oak, from the beautiful fall on the Owenmore river. It was afterwards called *Baile-easa-dara* [Ballyassadara], F. M., the town of Assdara, which has been shortened to the present name.

Ballysaggart; the town of the *sagart* or priest.

Ballysakeery in Mayo; see page 3.

Ballysallagh; dirty town.

Ballyshane; Shane's or John's town.

Ballyshannon: the old ford on the Erne is called by the annalists *Ath-seanaigh* and *Bel-atha-seanaigh* [Bellashanny]; from the latter, the present name is derived, and it means the mouth of *Seanach's* or *Shannagh's* ford, a man's name in common use. The *on* is a modern corruption; the peasantry call the town *Ballyshanny*, which is nearer the original. Ballyshannon in Kildare is similarly derived.

Ballytarsna, Ballytarsney; cross-town; i. e. the village or townland had a *cross* or transverse position.

Ballyteige; O'Teige's town.

Ballytrasna; same as Ballytarsna.

Ballyvaghan in Clare; *Baile-ui-Bheachain*, O'Behan's town.

Ballywater; *Baile-uachtar*, upper town.

Ballywillin; the town of the mill (*muileann*).

Balrath; *Baile-ratha*, the town of the fort.

Balrathboyne in Meath. St. *Baeithin* [Bweeheen; but

often pron. Boyne], the son of *Cuana*, built a church here near an ancient rath, and the rath remains, though the church is gone. Hence it was called *Rath-Baeithin*, and in recent times, Balrathboyne, the town of *Baeithin's* rath.

Balrothery; *Baile-a'-ridire* [Ballyariddery], the town of the knight.

Baltinglass; it is written *Bealach-Chonglais* [Ballaconglas] in Irish authorities, the road or pass of *Cuglas*, a person about whom there is a very ancient legend.

Baltrasna; the same as Ballytarsna.

Baltray; the town of the strand (*traigh*).

Banagh, barony of, in Donegal. It is called in the annals *Baghaineach* [Bawnagh], i. e. the territory of *Boghaine* [Boana] or *Enna Boghaine*, the son of Conall Gulban, son of the great king Niall of the Nine Hostages, who reigned from A. D 379 to 405.

Banagher and Bangor; *Beannchor* [Banaher], F. M., (from the root *beann*), signifies horns, or pointed hills or rocks, and sometimes simply a pointed hill.

Bannow in Wexford; the harbour was called *Cuan-an-bhainbh* [Coon-an-wonniv], the harbour of the *bonniv* or sucking pig; and the village has preserved the latter part of the name changed to Bannow.

Bansha; *Bainseach* [Bawnsha], a level place.

Bantry; *Beantraighe* [Bantry], Book of R., i. e. the descendants of *Beann* [Ban], one of the sons of Conor Mac Nessa, king of Ulster in the first century. A part of the tribe settled in Wexford, and another part in Cork, and the barony of Bantry in the former county, and the town of Bantry in the latter, retain their name.

Barna; *Bearna*, a gap.

Barnaboy; yellow gap.

Barnageeha, Barnageehy; windy gap (*gaoth*).

Barnane-Ely in Tipperary; from the remarkable gap in the Devil's Bit mountain; *Bearnán-Eile*, the little gap of Ely, the ancient territory in which it was situated.

Barnes, Barnish; *Bearnas*, a gap.

Barnismore; great gap.

Barr; the top of anything.

Baslick; *Baisleac*, F. M., a *basilica* or church.

Batterstown; the town of the *batter* (*bóthar*) or road.

Bawnmore; great green field.

Bawnoge; little green field.

Bawnreagh; greyish green field.

Baunskeha; the green field of the bush (*sceach*).

Bawnboy; yellow field.

Bawnfune; *Bán-fionn*, white field.

Bawnmore; great green field.

Beagh; *Beitheach* [Beha], a place of birches.

Bear; barony, island, and haven, in Cork.   Owen
More, king of Munster in the second century, spent
nine years in Spain, and, according to an old legend, he
married *Beara*, daughter of the king of that country.
On his return to Ireland to make war against Conn
of the hundred battles, he landed on the north side
of Bantry bay, and called the place *Beara* in honour
of his wife.

Beheenagh, Behernagh; a place of birches (*beith*).

Behy; birch land.

Belfarsad; the same as Belfast.

Belfast.   In old times the Lagan used to be crossed here
by a *farset* or sandbank, and hence the place was
called *Belfeirste*, F. M., the *bel* or ford of the *farset*.

Bellaghy; the mouth or entrance of the *lahagh* or
slough.

Bellanacargy in Cavan; *Bel-atha-na-cairrge*, the mouth
of the ford of the rock (*carraig*).

Bellanagar in Roscommon; *Bel-atha-na-gcarr*, the mouth
of the ford of the cars.

Bellananagh in Cavan; *Bel-atha-na-neach*, the mouth of
the ford of the horses (*each*).

Bellaugh in Roscommon; the same as Bellaghy.

Belleek near Ballyshannon; *Bel-leice* [Bellecka], F. M.,
the ford-mouth of the flag stone, from the flat sur-
faced rock in the bed of the river.   Belleek in other
places is similarly derived.

Beltany ; from *Bealtaine* or *Beltaine*, the first of May;
because the May day sports used to be celebrated there.

Ben; a peak, a pointed hill (*beann*).

Benbo mountain near Manorhamilton, is called in Irish *Beanna-bo*, F. M., the peaks or horns of the cow, from its curious double peak.

Benburb in Tyrone; from a cliff over the Blackwater, called in the annals *Beann-borb*, the proud peak.

Bengore head; the peak of the goats *(gabhar)*.

Bengorm; blue peak.

Benmore; great peak.

Bignion or Binnion; small *ben* or peak.

Billy in Antrim; *Bilĕ*, an ancient tree.

Binbulbin; correct name, *Binn-Gulbain*, Gulban's peak.

Bogagh, Boggagh, Boggan, Boggaun; a boggy place.

Boher; *Bothar* [bōher], a road.

Boherard; high road.

Boherboy; yellow road.

Boherduff; see page 2.

Bohereen; little road.

Bohermeen; smooth road.

Boherroe; red road.

Boho in Fermanagh; *Botha* [boha], tents or huts.

Bohola; *Both-Thola*, Hy. F., *St. Tola's* hut.

Boley; *buaile*, a milking place for cattle.

Boleybeg; little *boley* or dairy place.

Boola, booley; the same as Boley.

Boolyglass; green *booley*.

Booterstown near Dublin; the town of the *bothar, batter*, or road. In a roll of the fifteenth century it is called *Ballybothyr*, which shows that the Irish name was *Baile-an-bhothair*, the town of the road, of which the present name is a kind of half translation.

Borheen; same as Bohereen.

Borris; *Buirghes* [burris], a burgage or borough.

Borris-in-Ossory; from the old territory of Ossory.

Borrisokane; O'Keane's borough town.

Borrisoleigh; from the ancient territory *Ui Luighdheach* [Hy Leea], in which it was situated.

Bourney in Tipperary; *Boirne* [bourny], rocky lands, the plural of *Burren*.

Bovevagh; *Both-Mheidhbhe* [Boh-veva], the hut or tent of Maev or Mabel, a woman's name.

Boylagh, barony of, in Donegal; i. e. the territory of the O'Boyles.

Boyounagh; yellow *ounagh* or marsh (*abhnach*).

Braade; same as Braid.

Brackagh, Brackenagh, Brackernagh, Bracklagh; a speckled place, from *breac*, speckled.

Bracklin, Brackloon; *Breac-cluain*, speckled meadow.

Braid, the, in Antrim; applied to the deep glen through which the river flows; *Braghad* [braud], a gullet or gorge.

Brandon hill in Kerry, and also in Kilkenny; both called from St. Brendan the Navigator, who flourished in the sixth century.

Bray in Wicklow: it is called Bree in old documents, and it took name from the rocky head near it: *Bri* [bree], a hill. The name of Bray head in Valentia Island in Kerry, is similarly derived.

Breaghva, Breaghwy, Breaghy; *Breach-mhagh* [Breavah], the plain of the wolves (*breach*, a wolf; *magh*, a plain).

Breandrum; stinking *drum* or ridge.

Brigown near Mitchelstown in Cork; written *Bri-gobhunn* [Breegown] in the Book of Lismore, the *bree* or hill of the smith (*gobha*).

Brittas; speckled land.

Britway in Cork; a corruption of *Breaghva*, which see.

Brockagh; a place of *brocs* or badgers.

Bruff in Limerick; a corrupt form of *Brugh* [bru], a fort or mansion. The *brugh* is the old fort near the town.

Bruis; another form of *Brugh* [bru], a mansion.

Bruree in Limerick; called in Irish documents *Brughrigh* [Bruree], the fort or palace of the king; for it was the chief seat of Olioll Olum, king of Munster in the second century, and afterwards of the O'Donovans. Several of the old forts still remain.

Bullaun; *Bullán*, a well in a rock.

Bun; the bottom or end of anything; the mouth of a river.

Buncrana; the mouth of the river Crana.

Bunlahy; the end of the *lahagh* or slough.

Bunratty in Clare; the mouth of the river Ratty, now called the Owen O'Garney.

Burren; *Boireann,* a rock, a rocky district.

Burriscarra; the *burris* or borough of the old territory
of Carra.

Burrishoole; derived like Burriscarra, from the territory
of *Umhall* [ool] or " The Owles."

Burrisnafarney in Tipperary; the *burris* or borough of
the alder-plain (see Farney).

Buttevant in Cork; from the French motto of the
Barrys, *Boutez-en-avant,* push forward. The Irish
name is Kilnamullagh, the *cell* or church of the summits (*mullach*).

Cabragh; bad land.

Caher; *cathair* [caher], a circular stone fort.

Caherbarnagh; gapped *caher* or fort: (*bearnach,* gapped).

Caherconlish in Limerick; *Cathair-chinn-lis,* the *caher*
at the head of the *lis* or fort.

Caherduggan; Duggan's *caher* or stone fort.

Cahergal; white *caher* or stone fort.

Caherkeen in Cork ; beautiful *caher* or fort.

Cahersiveen in Kerry: it exactly preserves the pronunciation of the Irish name *Cathair-Saidhbhin,* the stone
fort of *Saidhbhin,* or Sabina, a woman's name.

Cahirconree mountain near Tralee; *Curoi's* caher, i. e.
the celebrated chief, *Curoi Mac Daire,* who flourished
in the first century. His caher still remains on a
shoulder of the mountain.

Caldragh; *Cealdrach,* an old burying ground.

Callow; *Cala,* a marshy meadow along a river.

Callowhill; *Collchoill,* hazel wood (*coll* and *coill*).

Caltragh; same as Caldragh.

Calluragh; *Ceallurach,* an old burial ground.

Camas, Camus; anything that winds, a winding stream:
from *cam,* crooked.

Camlin; crooked line; often applied to a river.

Camlough ; crooked lake (*cam* and *loch*).

Cappa, Cappagh; *ceapach,* a plot of land laid down for
tillage.

Cappaghbeg; little tillage-plot.

Cappaghmore, Cappamore; great tillage-plot.

Cappaghwhite in Tipperary; White's tillage-plot.

Capparoe; red plot.

Cappog, Cappoge; little *cappagh* or plot.

Cappoquin; *Ceapach-Chuinn,* Conn's tillage-plot.

Caran, Caraun ; a rocky place (from *carr*).

Carbury baronies in Longford and Sligo; so called because they were inhabited by the descendants of Carbery, one of the sons of Niall of the Nine Hostages, king of Ireland from A. D. 379 to 405.

Cargagh ; a rocky place (from *carraig*).

Cargan, Cargin; a little rock, a rocky place.

Carha; *Cairthe* [carha], a pillar stone.

Carhoo ; *ceathramhadh* [carhoo], a quarter (of land).

Carlingford ; *ford* is the Danish *fiord,* a sea inlet; the old Irish name is *Cairlinn ;* Carlingford, the *fiord* of *Cairlinn.*

Carlow; called in Irish documents *Cetherloch* [Caherlough], quadruple lake (*cether,* four); the Barrow anciently formed four lakes there.

Carn ; a monumental heap of stones.

Carnacally; the carn of the hag (*cailleach*).

Carnalbanagh ; the carn of the *Albanach* or Scotchman.

Carnaun; little carn or monumental heap.

Carnbane ; white carn (*ban* [bawn], white).

Carndonagh in Innishowen ; so called because the carn was situated in the parish of Donagh.

Carnew ; *Carn-Naoi* [Nee], Naoi's carn.

Carnglass; green carn.

Carnlough; the carn of the lake.

Carnmore; great carn.

Carnsore Point.   The old Irish name is *carn,* a monumental heap; the termination *ore* is Danish, and signifies the sandy point of a promontory : Carnsore is merely Carn's *ore,* the *ore* or sandy point of the carn.

Carnteel in Tyrone; *Carn-tSiadhail* [Carn-teel], F. M., *Siadhal's* or Shiel's carn (*s* eclipsed).

Carn Tierna near Fermoy.   *Tighernach* [Tierna] *Tetbannach,* king of Munster in the first century, was buried under the great carn which still remains on the top of the hill; and hence the name, signifying Tierna's carn.

Carntogher hills in Londonderry ; the carn of the *togher* or causeway.

Carrantuohill, the highest mountain in Ireland. It descends on the Killarney side by a curved edge, which the spectator catches in profile, all jagged and serrated with great masses of rock projecting like teeth. *Tuathail* [thoohil] means left-handed, and is applied to anything reversed from its proper direction; *carrán* is a reaping hook; and Carrantuohill is "the reversed reaping hook," because the teeth are on a convex instead of a concave edge.

Carrick; a rock, Irish *carraig* [carrig].

Carrickbeg; little rock.

Carrickduff; black rock.

Carrickfergus; Fergus's rock.

Carrickmore; great rock.

Carrick-on-Shannon. Carrick is here a corruption of *carra*, a weir; and the place took its name from an ancient weir across the Shannon. Its old anglicised name was Carrickdrumrusk, properly Carra-Drumrusk, the weir of Drumrusk.

Carrick-on-Suir; the rock of the Suir; from a large rock in the bed of the river.

Carrig; a rock, the same as Carrick.

Carrigafoyle on the Shannon, near Ballylongford; *Carraig-a'-phoill*, the rock of the hole; from a deep hole in the river, near the castle.

Carrigaholt in Clare; written by the F. M., *Carraig-an-chobhlaigh* [Carrigahowly], the rock of the fleet; and it took its name from the rock which rises over the bay where the fleets anchored. The local pronunciation of the Irish name is Carrigaholty, from which the present name is derived. Another place of the same name which preserves the correct pronunciation, is Carrigahowly on Newport bay in Mayo, the castle of the celebrated Grace O'Malley.

Carrigaline in Cork; the rock of O'Lehane.

Carrigallen in Leitrim; *Carraig-áluinn*, beautiful rock; from the rock on which the original church was built.

Carrigan, Carrigane; little rock.

Carrigans; little rocks.

Carrigdownane; Downan's or Downing's rock

Carrigeen; little rock : Carrrigeens; little rocks.

Carrignavar in Cork; see page 3.

Carrigogunnell near the Shannon in Limerick; *Carraig-O-gCoinneli*, F. M., the rock of the O'Connells.

Carrigroe; red rock.

Carrow; a quarter (of land).   See Carhoo.

Carroward; high quarter-land.

Carrowbane, Carrowbaun ; white quarter-land.

Carrowbeg; little quarter-land.

Carrowcrin ; the quarter-land of the tree (*crann*).

Carrowduff; black quarter-land.

Carrowgarriff, Carrowgarve ; rough quarter (*garbh,* rough).

Carrowkeel; narrow quarter (*cael,* narrow).

Carrowmanagh ; middle quarter-land.

Carrowmore ; great quarter-land.

Carrownaglogh ; the quarter of the stones (*cloch*).

Carrownamaddoo, Carrownamaddra, Carrownamaddy ; the quarter of the dogs (*madadh*, and *madradh*).

Carrowntober ; the quarter-land of the well (*tobar*).

Carrowreagh, Carrowrevagh ; grey quarter (*riabhach*).

Carrowroe ; red quarter-land.

Cartron ; an Anglo-Norman word, meaning a quarter of land.

Cashel : all the places of this name, including Cashel in Tipperary, were so called from a *caiseal* [cashel] or circular stone fort.

Cashen river *; casán* a path; for this river was, as it were, the high road into Kerry.

Cashlan; *Caislen*, a castle.

Castlebane, Castlebaun ; white castle.

Castlebar in Mayo ; shortened from Castle-Barry ; for it belonged to the Barrys after the English invasion.

Castlecomer ; the castle of the river-confluence (*comar*)

Castleconnell near Limerick : see page 3.

Castledermot in Kildare.   The old name was Disert-dermot, Diarmad's *desert* or hermitage, from Diarmad son of the king of Ulidia, who founded a monastery there about A. D. 800.   The present form of the name is derived from a castle built there by Walter de Riddlesford in the time of Strongbow.

Castledillon in Kildare; Irish name *Disert-Iolladhan* [Disertillan], *Iolladhan'* or Illan's hermitage; and the word Castle was substituted for Disert as in last name.

Castlelyons in Cork; the castle of O'Lehane or Lyons.

Castlemoyle; bald or dilapidated castle (*mael*).

Castlepook; the castle of the *pooka* or spright.

Castlerahan; the castle of the little rath or fort.

Castlereagh; grey castle (*riabhach*).

Castleterra in Cavan; a corruption from the Irish *Cos-a'-tsiorraigh* [Cussatirry], the foot(*cos*) of the *searrach* or foal. The name is accounted for by a legend about a stone with the print of a colt's foot on it.

Castleventry in Cork; the Irish name is *Caislean-na-gaeithe* [Cashlaunnageeha], the castle of the wind, of which the present name is a kind of translation.

Cavan; *Cabhan*, a hollow place. In some parts of Ulster it is understood to mean a hard round hill.

Cavanacaw; the round hill of the chaff (*cáth*); from the practice of winnowing.

Cavanaleck; the hill of the flag-stone.

Cavanreagh; grey hill (*riabhach* [reagh] grey).

Celbridge in Kildare; the *cell*, *kill*, or church, of the bridge; a kind of half translation from the original Irish name *Cill-droichid* [Kildrohed], the church of the *drohed* or bridge, which is still retained as the name of the parish, but shortened to Kildrought.

Cheek Point on the Suir below Waterford; a corruption of *Sheega* Point, the Irish name being *Pointe-na-sige*, the point of the *sheegas* or fairies.

Claggan; *Claigeann*, the skull, a round hill.

Clankee, barony of, in Cavan; *Clann-an-chaoich* [*Clann-an-kee*], the *clan* or descendants of the one-eyed man. They derived this cognomen from Niall O'Reilly, slain in 1256, who was called *caech* [kee], i. e. one-eyed.

Clanmaurice, barony of, in Kerry; the *clan* or descendants of Maurice Fitzgerald.

Clanwilliam, baronies of, in Limerick and Tipperary; the *clan* or descendants of William Burke.

Clara, Claragh; a level place; from *clar*.

Clare; a level piece of land (*clar*).

Clareen; little *clar* or level plain.

Clare-Galway. Irish name *Baile-an-chlair* [Ballinclare], F. M., the town of the plain; of which only the latter part is retained: called Clare-Galway to distinguish it from other Clares.

Clash; *Clais*, a trench or furrow.

Clashduff; black trench.

Clashganniff, Clashganniv, Clashganny; the trench of the sand, i. e. a sandpit (*gainimh* [ganniv], sand).

Clashmore; great trench.

Cleenish; *Claen-inis* [Cleeninish], sloping *inis* or island.

Cleggan; the same as Claggan.

Clifden in Galway; a very modern corruption of the Irish name *Clochán*, which signifies a beehive-shaped stone house.

Cliffs of Moher. The term *Mothar* [Moher] is applied in the south of Ireland to the ruin of a *caher*, *rath*, or fort; and on a cliff near Hag's Head there stands an old stone fort, called Moher O'Ruan, O'Ruan's ruined fort, from which the cliffs of Moher received their name.

Clogh; a stone; often applied also to a stone castle.

Cloghan, Cloghane, Cloghaun; a row of stepping stones across a river (from *cloch*).

Cloghbally; stony *bally* or townland.

Cloghboley, Cloghboola; stony *booley* or dairy place.

Cloghbrack; speckled stone.

Cloghcor; rough stone.

Clogheen; little stone or stone castle.

Clogher; generally applied to stony land—a place full of stones; but occasionally it means a rock.

Clogherbrien in Kerry; *Braen's* stony place.

Cloghereen; a place full of stones (*cloch*).

Cloghermore; great stony place.

Cloghernagh, Clogherny; a stony place.

Cloghfin; *Cloch-finn*, white stone.

Cloghineely in Donegal; *Cloch-Chinnfhaelaidh* [Clogh-Kineely], F. M., Kineely's or Mac Kineely's stone. Name accounted for by a long legend. The stone which gave name to the district is still preserved.

Cloghoge; a stony place.

Cloghpook; the *pooka's* or spright's stone.

Cloghran; *Cloichreán,* a stony place.

Cloghvoley, Cloghvoola, Cloghvoolia, Cloghvoula; *Cloch-bhuaile,* stony *booley* or dairy place.

Cloghy; a stony place.

Clogrennan; *Cloch-grianáin,* the stone castle of the *grianan* or summer residence.

Clomantagh in Kilkenny; Mantagh's stone castle.

Clon; a meadow. See Cloon.

Clonad; *Cluain-fhada* [Cloonada], long meadow

Clonagh; *Cluain-each,* horse meadow.

Clonallan in Down; called by Colgan and others *Cluain-Dallain,* Dallan's meadow; from Dallan Forgall, a celebrated poet of the sixth century.

Clonalvy; *Cluain-Ailbhe, Ailbhe's* or Alvy's meadow.

Clonamery; the meadow of the *iomaire* or ridge.

Clonard in Meath; written in Irish authorities *Cluain-Eraird,* Erard's meadow. There are several other places called Clonard and Cloonard; but in these the Irish form is probably *Cluain-ard,* high meadow.

Clonarney; *Cluain-airne,* the meadow of sloes.

Clonaslee; the meadow of the *slighe* [slee] or road.

Clonbeg; little meadow.

Clonbrock; the meadow of the *brocs* or badgers.

Cloncrew in Limerick; *Cluain-creamha* [crawa], the meadow of wild garlick.

Cloncullen; holly meadow.

Cloncurry; shortened from *Cluain-Conaire* [Cloon-Conary], F. M., Conary's meadow.

Clondalkin near Dublin; *Cluain-Dolcain,* Dolcan's meadow.

Clonduff in Down; *Cluain-daimh* [dav], O'C. Cal., the meadow of the ox.

Clone; a meadow; same as Clon and Cloon.

Cloneen; little meadow.

Clonegall in Carlow; *Cluain-na-nGall* [Cloon-nung-aul], the meadow of the *Galls* or foreigners.

Clonenagh in Queen's County; *Cluain-eidhnech* [ēnagh], O'C. Cal., the meadow of ivy (see *eidhneán* in Vocab.). It was so called before the sixth century, and to this day it abounds in ivy.

Clones (pronounced in two syllables); *Cluain-Eois* [Cloonoce], F. M., the meadow of *Eos* [Oce], a man's name.

Clonfad, Clonfadda, and Cloonfad; *Cluain-fada*, long meadow.

Clonfeacle in Tyrone; called *Cluain-fiacla* [feckla] in the Book of Leinster; the meadow of the tooth.

Clonfert: the Book of Leinster writes the name *Cluain-ferta*, the meadow of the grave.

Clongill; *Cluain-Gaill*, the meadow of the foreigner.

Clongowes; the meadow of the smith (*gobha*).

Clonkeen; *Cluain-caein* [keen], beautiful meadow.

Clonlea, Clonleigh, and Cloonlee; *Cluain-laegh* [lee], the meadow of the calves.

Clonliff; the meadow of herbs (*lubh*, an herb).

Clonmacnoise; written in Irish documents of the eighth century *Cluain-maccu-Nois*, which was the old pagan name; and it signifies the meadow of the sons of *Nos.* This *Nos* was the son of *Fiudhach* [Feeagh], a chief of the tribe of *Dealbhna* or Delvin, in whose territory Clonmacnoise was situated.

Clonmeen; *Cluain-min* [meen], smooth meadow.

Clonmel; *Cluain-meala* [malla], the meadow of honey (*mil*).

Clonmellon; *Cluain-milain*, F. M., Milan's meadow.

Clonmelsh; *Cluain-milis*, sweet meadow (from honey).

Clonmore; great meadow.

Clonmult; the meadow of the wethers (*molt*).

Clonoghil; the meadow of the yew-wood (*eóchaill*).

Clonoulty; *Cluain-Ultaigh* [ulty], the Ulsterman's meadow.

Clonshire; *Cluain-siar*, western meadow.

Clonsilla; *Cluain-saileach*, the meadow of sallows.

Clonskeagh; *Cluain-sceach*, the meadow of the white thorns.

Clontarf; *Cluain-tarbh* [tarriv], F. M., the meadow of the bulls.

Clontibret; written by the annalists *Cluain-tiobrat*, the meadow of the spring (*tipra*, same as *tobar*).

Clonturk, and Cloonturk; the boar's meadow (*torc*).

Clonty: same as Cloonty, which see.

Clonygowan; *Cluain-na-ngamhan* [*Cloon-nung-own*], F. M., the meadow of the calves.

Clonyhurk; *Cluain-da-thorc* [Cloonahork], F. M., the meadow of the two boars.

Cloon, and Cloone; a meadow. See *Cluain* in Vocabulary.

Cloonagh; the meadow of horses (*each*).

Cloonard. See Clonard.

Cloonawillin; *Cluain-a'-mhuilinn*, the meadow of the mill.

Cloonbeg; little meadow.

Clooncah; the meadow of the battle (*cath*).

Clooncoose, Clooncose; *Cluain-cuas*, F. M., the meadow of the caves.

Clooncraff; same as Cloncrew.

Clooncunna, Clooncunnig, Clooncunny; the meadow of the firewood (*conadh*).

Cloondara; *Cluain-da-rath*, F. M., the meadow of the two raths or forts.

Cloonee and Clooney; meadow land.

Clooneen; little meadow.

Cloonfinlough; the meadow of the clear lake.

Cloonkeen; *Cluain-caein*, beautiful meadow.

Cloonlara; the meadow of the mare (*lárach*).

Cloonlougher; the meadow of the rushes (*luachra*).

Cloonmore; great meadow.

Cloonnagashel in Mayo. See page 2.

Cloonshannagh, Cloonshinnagh; fox meadow (*sionnach*).

Cloonshee; the meadow of the fairies (*sidh*).

Cloonsillagh; the meadow of sallows.

Cloonteen; little meadow.

Cloonties; *Cluainte*, meadows (English plural form).

Cloontubbrid; same as Clontibret.

Cloontuskert; *Cluain-tuaisceirt* [tooskert], F. M., northern meadow.

Cloonty; *Cluainte*, meadows, plural of *cluain*.

Cloran, Clorane, Clorhane; a stony place (*cloch*).

Clough; a stone or stone castle.

Cloyne in Cork; shortened from *Cluain-uamha* [Cloon-oóa], as it is written in the Book of Leinster. The

name signifies the meadow of the cave (*uaimh*); and
the cave is still to be seen.

Clyduff; black dyke or mound (*cladh*).

Colehill; *Coll-choill*, hazel wood.

Coleraine. We are told in the Tripartite Life of St.
Patrick, that a chieftain named Nadslua presented
the saint with a piece of land on the bank of the
river Bann, on which to build a church. It was a
spot overgrown with ferns, and it happened at the
moment that some boys were amusing themselves by
setting them on fire. Hence the place was called
Cuil-rathain [Coolrahen], which Colgan translates
Secessus filicis, the corner (*cuil*) of the ferns. Cool-
rain, Coolrainey and Coolrahnee, are similarly derived.

Collon; a place of hazels (*coll*).

Colp near Drogheda. According to an ancient legend,
when the Milesian brothers invaded Ireland, one of
them, Colpa the swordsman, was drowned at the
mouth of the Boyne; hence it was called Inver-
Colpa, Colpa's river mouth; and the parish of Colp,
on its southern bank, retains the latter part of the
name a little shortened.

Comber, Comer; see page 4.

Commaun; a little *cum* or hollow.

Conicar, Conicker, Conigar, Coneykeare; *Cuinicér* [cun-
nikere], a rabbit warren.

Conlig; the *liag* or stone of the hounds (*cu*).

Connello, baronies of, in Limerick. This was the an-
cient territory of the tribe of Hy Conall or *Hy
Conaill Gabra* [Goura] (so written in the Book of
Leinster), who were descended and named from
Conall, the ninth in descent from Olioll Olum, king
of Munster in the second century.

Connemara. Maev, queen of Connaught in the time
of Conor mac Nessa, had three sons by Fergus mac
Roy, ex-king of Ulster, namely, *Ciar* [Keer], *Conmac*, and *Modhruadh* [Mōroo]. The descendants of
Conmac were called *Conmacnĕ* (*ne*, a progeny), and
they were settled in Connaught, where they gave
name to several territories. One of these, viz., the

district lying west of Lough Corrib and Lough Mask, from its situation near the sea, was called, to distin tinguish it from the others, *Conmacnĕ-mara* (O'Dugan: *muir*, the sea, gen. *mara*), or the sea-side *Conmacne*, which has been shortened to the present name Connemara.

Connor in Antrim; written *Condeire* or *Condaire* in various authorities; the *derry* or oak wood of the dogs (*cu*), or as it is explained in a gloss in the Martyrology of Aengus, "The oak wood in which were wild dogs formerly, and she wolves used to dwell therein."

Convoy, Conva; *Con-mhagh*, hound plain (*cu* and *magh*).

Conwal; *Congbhail* [Congwal], F. M., a habitation.

Cooga, Coogue; *Coigeadh* [Cōga], a fifth part.

Cool, Coole; *cuil*, a corner, or *cul*, a back.

Coolattin; the corner of the furze (*aiteann*).

Coolavin, a barony in Sligo; *Cuil-O'bhFinn* [Coolovin], F. M., the corner or angle of the O'Finns.

Coolbanagher; the angle of the pinnacles.   (See Banagher.)

Coolbane, Coolbaun; white corner or back.

Coolcashin; Cashin's corner or angle.

Coolderry; back *derry* or oak word.

Cooleen, little corner; Cooleeny, little corners.

Cooleeshal, Coolishal; low corner (*iseal*).

Cooley hills near Carlingford.   After the defeat of the Tuatha De Dananns by the Milesians, at Teltown in Meath, the Milesian chief *Cuailgne* [Cooley], following up the pursuit, was slain here; and the district was called from him, *Cuailgne*, which name is still applied to the range of hills.

Coolgreany; sunny corner or back (*grian* the sun).

Coolhill and Coolkill; *cúl-choill*, back wood.

Coolnahinch; the corner of the *inis*, island, or river meadow.

Coolock, Coologe; little corner or angle.

Coolroe; red corner or back.

Coom, Coombe; *cúm*, a hollow or mountain valley.

Coomnagoppul at Killarney; *Cum-na-geapall*, the hollow or valley of the horses; from the practice of sending horses to graze in it.

Coomyduff near Killarney; *Cum-ui-Dhuibh* [Coomywiv], O'Duff's valley; usually but erroneously translated Black valley.

Coos, Coose; *cuas*, a cave.

Coosan, Coosane, Coosaun; little cave.

Cor, Corr. This word has several meanings, but it generally signifies a round hill.

Corballis, Corbally; odd townland: *cor* here means odd.

Corbeagh; round hill of the birch (*beith*).

Corcomohide in Limerick; *Corca-Muichet* (Book of Lismore), the race (*corca*) of *Muichet*, one of the disciples of the druid, *Mogh Ruith*.

Corcomroe, barony of, in Clare; *Corca-Modhruadh* or *Corcomruadh* [Corcomrua: Book of Leinster], the race (*corca*) of *Modhruadh*, son of queen Maev. (See Connemara.)

Corcreevy; branchy hill. *Craebh* [creeve], a branch.

Cordangan; fortified *cor* or round hill.

Cordarragh; round hill of the oak (*dair*).

Corduff; black round hill.

Corgarve; rough round hill (*garbh*).

Corglass; green round hill (*glas*).

Corick; the meeting of two rivers.

Cork; *Corcach*, a marsh. The city grew round a monastery founded in the sixth century on the edge of a marsh, by St. Finbar; and even yet a part of the city is called the Marsh.

Corkagh; the same name as Cork.

Corkaguiny, barony of, in Kerry; *Corca-Duibhne* (divny: O'Dugan], the race (*corca*) of *Duibhne*, son of Carbery Musc, who was son of Conary II., king of Ireland from A. D. 158 to 165. *D* changed to *g*: see page 4.

Corkaree, barony of, in Westmeath; *Corca Raeidhe* [Ree: O'Dugan], the race (*corca*) of *Fiacha Raidhe* [Feeha Ree], grandson of Felimy the Lawgiver, king of Ireland from A. D. 111 to 119.

Corkeeran, Corrakeeran; the round hill of the *keerans* or quicken trees (*caerthainn*).

Corkey; the same name as Cork and Corkagh.

Corlat; the round hill of the sepulchres (*leacht*).

Corlea; grey round hill.

Corlough; the lake of the *corrs* or herons.

Cormeen; smooth round hill.

Cornacreeve; the round hill of the branchy tree (*craebh*).

Cornagee, Cornageeha; the round hill of the wind (*gaeth*).

Cornahoe; the round hill of the cave (*uaimh*).

Cornamucklagh; the round hill of the piggeries. See Mucklagh.

Cornaveagh; the round hills of the ravens (*fiach*).

Corratober; the round hill of the well (*tobar*).

Corrinshigo, Corrinshigagh; the round hill of the ash trees. See *Fuinnse* in Vocabulary.

Corrofin in Clare; *Coradh-Finne* [Corrafinna], F. M., the weir of Finna, a woman's name.

Corskeagh; the round hill of the white thorns.

Coshbride, Coshlea, Coshma, baronies, the first in Waterford, the others in Limerick. Cosh (Irish *cois*, from *cos* a foot), means at the foot of, near, beside. Coshbride, the barony along the river Bride. Coshlea, *cois-shleibhe* [cushleva], at the foot of the *sliabh* or mountain, i. e. the Galties. Coshma, *Cois-Maighe* [ma], the barony along the river Maigue.

Craan, Craane; a stony place (from *carr*).

Crag, Craig; other forms of *carraig*, a rock.

Cran; *Crann*, a tree.

Cranfield; a corruption of *Creamh-choill* [Cravwhill], the wood (*coill*) of wild garlic (*creamh*).

Crannagh; a place abounding in *cranns* or trees.

Crannoge; a habitation on an artificial island in a lake.

Cranny; the same as Crannagh.

Cratloe, Crataloe; sallow wood.

Craughwell; *Creamh-choill*, wild garlic wood.

Crecora in Limerick; *Craebh-cumhraidhe* [Crave-coory] O'Dugan, sweet scented *creeve* or branchy tree.

Creevagh; a branchy place (*craebh*).

Creeve; *Craebh* [creeve], a branch, a branchy tree.

Creevelea; grey branch or branchy tree.

Creevy; the same as Creevagh.

Creg, Cregg; *Creag*, a rock.

Creggan, Creggane, Creggaun ; little rock, rocky ground.

Cremorne barony in Monaghan ; *Crioch - Mughdhorn* [Cree-Mourne], the country (*crioch*) of the tribe of *Mughdhorna* [Mourna], who were descended and named from *Mughdhorn* [Mourne], the son of Colla Meann, one of the three brothers who conquered Ulster, and destroyed the palace of Emania in A. D. 332.

Crew ; the same name as Creeve.

Croagh ; *Cruach*, a rick or stacked up hill.

Croaghan, Croaghaun ; a round or piled up hill.

Croaghpatrick ; St. Patrick's rick or hill.

Crock is very generally used in the northern half of Ireland instead of Knock, a hill.

Crockanure ; *Cnoc-an-iúbhair*, the hill of the yew.

Crogh ; the same as Croagh.

Croghan, Crohane ; the same as Croaghan.

Crossakeel ; slender crosses.

Crossan, Crossane, Crossaun ; little cross.

Crossboyne ; *Cros-Baeithin*, Hy F., *Baeithin's* or Boyne's cross.

Crosserlough ; the cross on (*air*) or near the lake.

Crossgar ; short cross.

Crossmaglen in Armagh ; *Cros-meg-Fhloinn* [Cros-meg-lin : *fh* silent], the cross of Flann's son.

Crossmolina in Mayo ; *Cros - ui-Mhaelfhina*, F. M., O'Mulleeny's or Mullany's cross.

Crossoge ; little cross.

Crossreagh ; grey cross (*riabhach*).

Crott ; *Cruit*, a hump, a humpy backed hill.

Cruagh ; the same as Croagh.

Cruit ; the same as Crott.

Crumlin, Cromlin ; *Cruim-ghlinn*, [Crumlin], F. M., curved glen.

Crusheen ; *Croisin*, little cross.

Cuilbeg, Cuilmore ; little wood, great wood (*coill*).

Culdaff ; *Cul-dabhach* [Culdava], the back (*cul*) of the flax-dam or pool.

Culfeightrin in Antrim ; *Cuil-eachtrann* [Coolaghtran], the corner (*cuil*) of the strangers.

Cullan, Cullane, Cullaun ; a place of hazels (*coll*)

Culleen ; *Coillín,* little wood.
Cullen ; *Cuillionn* [Cullen], holly, holly land.
Cullenagh ; a place producing holly.
Cullentra, Cullentragh ; same as Cullenagh.
Cullenwaine in King's County ; *Cuil-O-nDubhain* [Cool-ōnuan], F. M., the corner or angle of the O'Duanes.
Cullion ; the same as Cullen.
Cully ; woodland ; from *coill.*
Culmullen in Meath ; the angle of the mill.
Cumber, Cummer.   See page 4.
Curra, Curragh ; *currach,* generally a marsh ; sometimes a race course.
Currabaha, Currabeha ; the marsh of the birch.
Curraghbeg ; little marsh.
Curraghboy ; yellow marsh.
Curraghduff ; black marsh.
Curraghlahan, Curraghlane ; broad marsh.
Curraghmore ; great marsh.
Curragh of Kildare. The word here means a race course : the Curragh of Kildare has been used as a race course from the earliest ages.
Curraheen ; little *currach* or marsh.
Curry ; another form of Curragh, a marsh.
Cush.   See Coshbride.
Cushendall in Antrim ; *Cois-abhann-Dhalla* [Cush-oun-dalla], the foot or termination of the river Dall.
Cushendun in Antrim ; called by the F. M., *Bun-abhann-Duine,* the end, i. e. the mouth of the river Dun ; this was afterwards changed to *Cois-abhann-Duine* [Cush-oun-Dunny] by the substitution of *Cois,* the foot or end for *Bun.*
Cutteen ; *Coitchionn* [cutteen], common, a commonage.
Dalkey Island near Dublin. The Irish name is *Delginis* (O'C. Cal.), thorn island ; which the Danes, who had a fortress on it in the tenth century, translated to the present name, by changing *Delg* into their word *Dalk,* a thorn ; and substituting the northern word *ey,* an island, for *inis.*
Dangan ; *Daingean* [dangan], a fortress.
Dangandargan in Tipperary ; Dargan's fortress.
Darragh ; a place producing oaks (*dair*).

Darraragh, Darrery ; an oak forest, a place abounding in oaks (*Dairbhreach*).

Dawros; *Damhros*, the peninsula of oxen (*damh* and *ros*).

Deelis, Deelish ; *Duibh-lios* [Divlis], black *lis* or fort.

Delvin. There were formerly seven tribes called *Dealbhna* [Dalvăna], descended and named from *Lughaidh Dealbhaeth* [Lewy Dalway], who was the son of *Cas mac Tail* (seventh in descent from Olioll Olum : see Connello), the ancestor of the Dalcassians of Thomond : *Dealbhna*, i. e. *Dealbhaeth's* descendants. None of these have perpetuated their name except one, viz., *Dealbhna mor*, or the great *Dealbhna*, from whom the barony of Delvin in Westmeath received its name.

Dernish, Derinch, Derinish; oak island (*dair*).

Derrada, Derradd ; *Doire-fhada*, long oak grove.

Derragh ; the same as Darragh.

Derreen ; little *derry* or oak grove or wood.

Derreens, Derries ; oak groves.

Derry ; *Doire* [Derry], an oak grove or wood.

Derryad, Derryadda ; *Doire-fhada*, long oak wood.

Derrybane, Derrybawn ; whitish oak wood.

Derrybeg; little oak wood.

Derrycreevy; the oak wood of the branchy tree.

Derrydorragh, Derrydorraghy ; dark oak wood (*dorcha*)

Derryduff; black oak wood.

Derryfadda; long oak wood.

Derrygarriff, Derrygarve ; rough oak wood (*garbh*).

Derrylahan, Derrylane; broad oak wood (*leathan*).

Derrylea; grey oak wood.

Derrylough, Derryloughan; the oak wood of the lake.

Derrymore ; great oak wood.

Derrynahinch ; the oak wood of the island or river meadow (*inis*).

Derrynane in Kerry ; *Doire-Fhionain* [Derry-Eenane : *Fh* silent], the oak grove of St. Finan Cam, a native of Corkaguiny, who flourished in the sixth century.

Derrynaseer; the oak grove of the *saers* or carpenters.

Derryvullan in Fermanagh; *Doire-Maelain* [Derry-Velan : *M* aspirated], F. M., Maelan's oak grove.

Desert : *Disert,* a desert or hermitage.

Desertcreat; corrupted from *Disert-da-Chrioch* [Di-sert-ā-cree], F. M., the hermitage of the two ter-ritories.

Desertegny; Egnagh's hermitage.

Desertmartin; Martin's hermitage.

Desertmore; great desert or hermitage.

Desertserges in Cork; Saerghus's hermitage.

Devenish Island in Lough Erne; *Daimhinis* [Davinish], F. M., the island of the oxen (*damh*).

Diamor; written in the Dinnseanchus, *Diamar*, i. e., a solitude.

Dingle; from Dingin, another form of *Daingean*, a for-tress, by a change of *n* to *l* (see page 3). Called in the annals, *Daingean-ui-Chuis*, now usually written Dingle-I-Coush, the fortress of O'Cush, the ancient proprietor.

Dinish, Deenish; *Duibh-inis* [Divinish], black island.

Disert; the same as Desert.

Donabate; *Domhnach-a'-bhaid*, the church of the boat.

Donagh; *Domhnach* [Downagh], a church.

Donaghcloney in Down; the church of the *cluain* or meadow.

Donaghcumper in Kildare; the church of the *cummer* or confluence.

Donaghedy in Tyrone; *Domhnach-Chaeide* [Donaheedy], the church of St. Caidoc, a companion of St. Colum-banus.

Donaghmore; great church.

Donaghmoyne in Monaghan; *Domhnach-Maighin*, the church of the little plain.

Donard; high *dun* or fort.

Donegal. The Danes had a settlement there before the Anglo-Norman invasion; and hence it was called *Dun-na-nGall* [Doonagall], the fortress of the *Galls* or foreigners.

Doneraile in Cork; written in the Book of Lismore *Dun-air-àill*, the fortress on the cliff.

Donnybrook; *Domhnach-Broc*, St. Broc's church.

Donnycarney; *Cearnach's* or Carney's church.

Donohill; the fortress of the yew wood (*eóchaill*).

Donore; *Dun-uabhair* [Dunoor], F. M. the fort of pride.

Doogary; *Dubhdhoire* [Dooary], black derry or oak wood.

Doon; *Dún*, a fortress.

Doonan, Doonane; little *dun* or fort.

Doonard; high fort.

Doonass near Killaloe; *Dun-easa*, the fortress of the cataract, i. e. the great rapid on the Shannon.

Doonbeg; little fortress.

Doondonnell; Donall's fortress.

Dooneen; little fort.

Doonfeeny; the fort of Finna (a woman).

Doonisky, Dunisky; the fort of the water (*uisge*).

Doonooney; Una's fort.

Douglas; *Dubh-ghlaise*, black stream.

Down; a form of *Dun*, a fortress.

Downings; *Dooneens* or little forts.

Downpatrick takes its name from the large entrenched *dun* near the cathedral. In the first century this fortress was the residence of a warrior of the Red Branch Knights, called *Celtchair*, or Keltar of the battles, from whom it is called in Irish authorities, Dunkeltar. By ecclesiastical writers it is commonly called *Dun-da-leth-glas*, the fortress of the two broken locks (*glas*) or fetters. This long name was afterwards shortened to *Dun* or Down, which was extended to the county. The name of St. Patrick was added, to commemorate his connexion with the place.

Downs; *duns* or forts.

Dreen; *Draeighean* [dreean], the blackthorn.

Dreenagh; a place producing blackthorns.

Dreenan; blackthorn, a place of blackthorns.

Drehidtarsna in Limerick; cross bridge.

Dressoge, Dressogagh; a briery or bushy place.

Dresternagh, Dresternan, Dristernan; same as Dressoge.

Drim; a form of *druim*, a ridge.

Drimeen, Drimmeen; little ridge.

Drimna, Drimnagh; ridges, a place full of ridges or hills.

Drinagh, Drinaghan; a place producing *dreens* or blackthorns.

Drinan, Drinaun; the same as Dreenan.

Drishaghaun, Drishane, Drishoge; same as Dressoge.

Droghed; *Droichead*, a bridge.

Drogheda; *Droiched-atha* [Drohedaha], F. M., the bridge of the ford; from the ford across the Boyne, used before the erection of a bridge.

Drom; *Druim*, a ridge or long hill.

Dromada, Dromadda; long *drum* or ridge.

Drombeg, Drumbeg; small ridge.

Dromcolliher in Limerick; a corruption of *Druim-Coll-choille* [Drum-Collohill], the ridge of the hazel wood.

Dromdaleague in Cork; the ridge of the two *liags* or pillar stones.

Dromgarriff; rough ridge.

Dromin; same meaning as Drom.

Dromineer in Tipperary; *Druim-inbhir* [Druminver], the ridge of the *inver* or river mouth : because it is situated near where the Nenagh river enters Lough Derg.

Dromkeen; beautiful ridge.

Dromore; great ridge or long hill.

Dromtrasna; cross ridge.

Drum; *Druim*, a ridge or long hill.

Drumad; *Druim-fhada*, long ridge.

Dromadoon; the ridge of the *dun* or fort.

Drumahaire in Leitrim ; *Druim-da-ethiar* [Drum-a-ehir], F. M., the ridge of the two air-demons.

Drumanure; the ridge of the yew tree.

Drumany, Drummany; ridges, ridged land.

Drumard ; high ridge or long hill.

Drumatemple; the ridge of the temple or church.

Drumavaddy ; the ridge of the dog (*madadh*).

Drumballyroney; the ridge of O'Roney's town.

Drumbane, Drumbaun; white ridge.

Drumbarnet, the ridge of the gap (*bearna*).

Drumbo, Drumboe; *Druimbo*, F. M., the cow's ridge.

Drumbrughas; the ridge of the farm-house.

Drumcanon ; the ridge of the white-faced cow: *crann-fhionn* [canon], whitehead

Drumcar in Louth; *Druim-caradh* [Drumcara], F. M., the ridge of the weir.

Drumcliff in Sligo; *Drium-chliabh* [Drumcleev], F. M., the ridge of the baskets.

Drumcolumb; St. Columba's ridge.

Drumcondra; Conra's ridge.

Drumcrin; the ridge of the tree (*crann*).

Drumcrow; the ridge of the cattle sheds (*cro*).

Drumcullen, Drumcullion; the ridge of holly.

Drumderg; *Druim-dearg*, red ridge.

Drumduff; *Druim-dubh*, black ridge.

Drumfad; *Druim-fada*, long ridge.

Drumgill; the ridge of the *Gall* or foreigner.

Drumgoose, Drumgose; the ridge of the caves (*cuas*).

Drumgowna, Drumgownagh; *Druim-gamhnach*, the ridge of the heifers.

Drumharriff, Drumherriff; *Druim-thairbh* [Drum-harriv], the ridge of the bull.

Drumhillagh; see page 2.

Drumhirk; *Druim-thuirc*, the ridge of the boar.

Drumhome in Donegal. In O'C. Cal. the name is written *Druim-Thuama* [Drumhooma], and Adamnan translates it *Dorsum Tommae*, the ridge of Tomma, a pagan woman's name.

Drumillard, Drummillar; the eagle's ridge (*iolar*).

Drumkeen; beautiful ridge.

Drumkeeran; the ridge of the quicken trees.

Drumlane; *Druim-leathan* [lahan], F. M., broad ridge.

Drumlease; *Druim-lias*, the ridge of the huts.

Drumlish; the ridge of the *lis* or fort.

Drumlougher; the ridge of the rushes (*luachra*).

Drumman; same meaning as Drum.

Drummeen; little ridge.

Drummin; same meaning as Drum.

Drummond; a corrupt form of Drumman. See page 4.

Drummuck; the ridge of the pigs (*muc*).

Drummully; the ridge of the summit (*mullach*).

Drumnacross; the ridge of the cross.

Drumneen; little ridge.

Drumquin; *Druim-Chuinn*, Conn's ridge.

Drumraine, Drumrainy; ferny ridge (*ráthain*).

Drumreagh; *Druim-riabbach*, grey ridge.

Drumroe; *Druim-ruadh*, red ridge.

Drumroosk; the ridge of the *ruosk* or marsh.

Drumshallon; the ridge of the gallows (*sealan*).

Drumshanbo; the ridge of the old *both* or tent (*sean*, old).

Drumsillagh; see page 2.

Drumsna, Drumsnauv; *Druim-snamha* [snawa], the ridge of the swimming. See Lixnaw.

Drumsurn; the ridge of the furnace or kiln (*sorn*).

Duagh in Kerry; *Dubh-ath* [Dooah], black ford, from a ford on the river Feale.

Dublin. The name is written in the annals *Duibh-linn* [Duvlin], which, in some of the Latin Lives of the saints, is translated *Nigra therma,* black pool; it was originally the name of that part of the Liffey on which the city is built, and is sufficiently descriptive at the present day. In very early ages an artificial ford of hurdles was constructed across the Liffey, where the main road from Tara to Wicklow crossed the river; and the city that subsequently sprung up around it was called from this circumstance *Ath-cliath* [Ah-clee], F. M., the ford of hurdles, which was the ancient name of Dublin. This name is still used by speakers of Irish in every part of Ireland; but they join it to Bally—*Baile-atha-cliath* (which they pronounce *Blaa-clee*), the town of the hurdle ford.

Dufferin, barony of, in Down; *Dubh-thrian* [Duv-reen], F. M., the black *treen* or third part.

Duhallow in Cork; *Duthaigh-Ealla* [Doohy-alla], F. M., the district of the Allo, from the Blackwater river, a portion of which was anciently called the Allo.

Dulane in Meath; *Tuilen,* F. M., little *tulach* or hill.

Duleek in Meath; *Daimhliag* [Davleeg], O'C. Cal., stone house or church (*daimh,* a house, and *liag*).

Dunamase in Queen's County; should have been called Dunmask, for the Irish name is *Dun-Masg,* F. M., the fortress of *Masg,* who was one of the ancestors of the Leinster people.

Dunamon in Galway; so called from a castle of the same name on the Suck; but the name, which the annalists write *Dun-Iomgain,* Imgan's fort, was anciently applied to a *dun,* which is still partly preserved.

Dunboe in Derry ; the fortress of the cow.

Dunboyne; *Dun-Baeithin, Baeithin's* or Boyne's fort.

Duncannon ; Conan's fortress.

Duncormick ; Cormac's fortress.

Dundalk. The name was originally applied to the great
fortress now called the moat of Castletown, a mile
inland, which was the residence of *Cuchullin,* chief
of the Red Branch knights in the first century. *Dun-
Dealgan* [Dalgan], F. M., the fortress of *Delga,* a
Firbolg chief, who built it.

Dunderrow in Cork ; written *Dun-dermaigi* [Dundar-
wah] in the Book of Leinster, the fortress of the oak-
plain (see Durrow) ; and the large dun from which it
received the name is still in existence, half a mile
south of the village.

Dundonald in Down, Donall's fortress ; so called from
a fort that stands not far from the church.

Dundrum ; *Dun-droma,* F. M., the fortress on the ridge
or hill.

Duneane in Antrim ; written in the Felire of Aengus,
Dun-da-én [Dun-ā-ain], the fortress of the two birds.

Dunfanaghy; *Dun-Fionnchon* [Finahan], *Finchu's* fort.

Dungannon in Tyrone; *Dun-Geanainn* [Gannin], F. M.,
Geanan's or Gannon's fortress.

Dungarvan; *Dun-Garbhain,* F. M., Garvan's fortress.

Dunhill ; *Dun-aille,* the fortress of the cliff.

Dunkineely in Donegal ; *Dun-mhic-Chionnfhaelaidh*
[Dunvickaneely], Mackineely's fort.

Dunkit; *Ceat's* or Keth's fortress.

Dunleer in Louth. Old name *Land-léri* (Book of Leinster), the church (*land* or *lann*) of austerity. Present
name formed by substituting *dun* a fort for *lann.*

Dunluce castle near the Giant's Causeway ; *Dunlios,*
F. M., strong *lios* or fort. *Dun* is here an adjective,
meaning strong.

Dunmanway in Cork. Old name *Dun-na-mbeann* [Dun-
aman], F. M., the fortress of the gables or pinnacles.
The last syllable *way* is from *buidhe* yellow [bwee,
or with the *b* aspirated, wee] :—Dunmanway, the
fortress of the yellow pinnacles.

Dunmore ; great fort.

Dunmurry; *Dun-Muireadhaigh*, Murray's fort.

Dunquin in Kerry; *Dun-caein* [Dunkeen], F. M., beautiful fort.

Dunshaughlin in Meath. A church was founded here for bishop *Sechnall* or Secundinus, St. Patrick's nephew; and hence it was called *Domhnach-Seachnaill* [Donna-Shaughnill], F. M., the church of St. *Sechnall*, which has been shortened to the present name.

Duntryleague in Limerick. According to a passage in the Book of Lismore, a *dun* or palace was built here for Cormac Cas, son of Olioll Olum (see Connello); and his bed was supported by three *liagáns* or pillar stones, from which the place was called *Dun-tri-liag*, the fortress of the three *liags* or pillar stones.

Durrow in King's County, a favourite residence of St. Columbkille. Venerable Bede has a short passage in his Eccl. Hist. (lib. iii., cap. iv.), in which the original form and translation of this name are given:—
" Before he (Columba) passed over into Britain, he had built a noble monastery in Ireland, which, from the great number of óaks, is in the Scotic (Irish) language called *Dearmhagh* [Darwah], the field of the oaks" (*dair* and *magh*).

Dysart and Dysert; the same as Desert.

Dysartenos in Queen's County. St. Aengus the Culdee, who died in the year 824, built a cell for himself here; and hence the place was called *Disert-Aenghusa*, Aengus's hermitage.

Easky in Sligo; from the river :—*Iascach* [Eeska], fishy (from *iasg*, a fish).

Eden : *Eudon* [edan], the brow; a hill brow.

Edenderry; the hill brow of the oak wood.

Edenmore; great hill brow.

Edergole, Edergoole; see Addergoole.

Eglish; a church; same as Aglish.

Eighter; *Iochtar* [eeter], lower.

Eliogarty in Tipperary; a shortened form of Ely O'Fogarty (shortened by having the *f* aspirated and omitted: see page 2), O'Fogarty's *Ely*, so called from its ancient possessors the O'Fogartys. See Ely.

Elphin in Roscommon. St. Patrick founded a church

here near a spring, over which stood a large stone; and hence the place was called *Aill-finn*, which Colgan interprets the rock (*aill*) of the clear spring (*finn* white, clear).

Ely. The different tribes called *Eile* or Ely were so named from their ancestor *Eile*, the seventh in descent from *Cian*, son of Olioll Olum (see Connello).

Emlagh; *Imleach* [Imlagh], land bordering on a lake; and hence a marshy or swampy place.

Emly in Tipperary. St. *Ailbhe* founded his establishment here in the fifth century, on the margin of a lake, which has been only lately drained. The place is called in the Irish authorities *Imleach-iobhair* [yure], the lake-marsh of the yew tree.

Emlygrennan in Limerick; a corruption of the Irish name *Bile-Ghroidhnin* [Billa-Gryneen], Grynan's ancient tree.

Enagh, the name of twenty townlands. Sometimes *Aenach*, a fair; sometimes *Eanach*, a marsh.

Ennereilly in Wicklow; *Inbher-Daeile* [Invereela], F. M., the *inver* or mouth of the river formerly called the Deel, now the Pennycomequick.

Ennis; *inis*, an island; a meadow along a river.

Enniskeen; *Inis-caein* [keen], F. M., beautiful island or river meadow.

Enniskerry; *Ath-na-scairbhe* [Annascarvy], the ford of the *scarriff* or rough river-crossing; from an ancient stony ford where the old road crosses the river.

Enniskillen; *Inis-Cethlenn* [Kehlen], F. M., the island of *Kethlenn*, wife of Balor, the Fomorian king of Tory Island.

Ennistimon; *Inis-Diomain*, F. M., *Diaman's* river meadow.

Errigal; *Aireagal*, a habitation, a small church.

Errigal Keeroge in Tyrone; *Aireagal Dachiarog* [Dakeeroge], F. M., the church of St. *Dachiarog*.

Errigal Trough in Monaghan; the church of (the barony of) Trough.

Esker; *Eiscir*, a sandhill.

Eskeragh, Eskragh; a place full of *eskers*.

Ess, Essan, Essaun; a waterfall.

Estersnow in Roscommon; a strange corruption from the Irish *Disert-Nuadhan* (Nooan), F. M., the hermitage of *St. Nuadha* (Nooa). Disert is often corrupted to *ister, ester, tirs, tristle,* &c.

Faddan; *Feadan,* a small brook.

Faha, Fahy; an exercise green. See *Faithche* in Vocabulary.

Farnagh, Farnane, Farnoge; a place of *Fearns* [Farns], or alders.

Farney in Monaghan; *Fearnmhagh* (Farnvah), Book of R., the alder plain (*fearn* and *magh*).

Farran; *Fearann,* land.

Farset, Farsid; *Fearsad,* a sandbank in a river.

Fartagh, Fertagh; a place of graves (*feart*).

Fasagh, Fassagh; a wilderness (*Fásach*).

Fassadinin in Kilkenny; the *fasagh* or wilderness of, or near, the river Dinin.

Feagh; *Fiodhach* [Feeagh], a woody place (*fidh*).

Fearmore; great grass (*féur*) or grassy place.

Feddan; the same as Faddan.

Feenagh; *Fiodhnach* [Feenagh], woody (*fidh*); a woody place.

Feighcullen in Kildare; *Fiodh-Chuilinn,* F. M., Cullen's wood.

Fenagh; the same as Feenagh.

Fennor; *Fionnabhair* [Finner], F. M., white field.

Fermanagh; so called from the tribe of *Fir-Monach,* (O'Dugan), the men of *Monach,* who were originally a Leinster tribe, so named from their ancestor, *Monach,* fifth in descent from Cahirmore, monarch of Ireland from A. D. 120 to 123.

Fermoy in Cork; *Feara-muighe* [Farra-moy], O'Dugan, the men of the plain.

Fermoyle; *Formaeil,* a round hill.

Fernagh, Ferney; same as Farnagh.

Ferns; *Fearna* [Farna], F. M., alders, a place abounding in alders: English plural termination added.

Ferrard, barony of, in Louth; *Feara-arda* [Farra-arda], F. M., the men of the height, i. e. of Slieve Bregh.

Fethard; *Fiodh-ard* [Feeard], F. M., high wood.

Fews, baronies of, in Armagh; *Feadha* [Fā], F. M.,

woods; with the English plural termination added.
Fews in Waterford has the same origin.

Fiddan, Fiddane, Fiddaun; same as Faddan.

Fiddown in Kilkenny; *Fidh-duin* [Feedoon], F. M.,
the wood of the *dun* or fort.

Fingall, a district lying north of Dublin, in which the
Danes settled; and hence it was called *Fine-Gall*
(O'C. Cal.), the territory or tribe (*fine*) of the *Galls*
or foreigners.

Finglas; clear stream (*fionn*, white, clear; and *glaise*).

Finn river and lake in Donegal; *Loch-Finnë*, the lake
of *Finna*, a woman, about whom there is an interest-
ing legend. The river took its name from the lake.
See Origin and History of Irish Names of Places,
page 167.

Finnea in Westmeath; *Fidh-an-atha* [Fee-an-aha]
F. M., the wood of the ford.

Fintona; *Fionn-tamhnach* [Fintowna], F. M., fair coloured field.

Foil; *Faill*, a cliff.

Foilduff; black cliff.

Forenaght, Forenaghts, Fornaght, Farnaght; *For-
nocht*, a bare, naked, or exposed hill.

Formil, Formoyle, Formweel; same as Fermoyle.

Forth. The descendants of Ohy Finn *Fothart* [Fōhart],
brother of Conn of the hundred battles (king of Ireland from A. D. 123 to 158), were called *Fotharta*
[Fōharta], Book of R. Some of them settled in the
present counties of Wexford and Carlow, where the
two baronies of Forth still retain their name.

Foy, Foygh ; forms of *Faithche*. See Faha.

Foybeg, Foymore; little and great exercise green.

Foyduff ; black exercise green.

Foyle; same as Foil.

Freagh, Freugh *Fraech*, heath, a heathy place.

Freaghduff, Freeduff; black heath.

Freaghillan, Freaghillaun; heathy island (*oileán*).

Freshford; Irish name *Achadh-úr* (Book of Leinster),
which should have been translated *Freshfield: Achadh*
was mistaken for *ath*.

Freughmore, Freaghmore; great heath.

Funcheon ; *Fuinnseann* [Funshin], the ash tree: the
ash-producing river.

Funshin, Funshinagh, Funshog, Funshoge; a place
producing ash trees (*fuinnse*).

Galbally, Gallavally, Galvally, Galwally; English town;
Gall here means an Englishman.

Galboley, Galboola, Galbooley, Galwolie; a *booley* or
dairy place belonging to *Galls* or English people.

Gallagh; a place full of rocks or standing stones. See
Gall in Vocabulary.

Gallan, Gallane ; *Gallan*, a standing stone.

Gallen. The descendants of *Cormac Gaileng*, great
grandson of Olioll Olum (see Connello), were called
Gailenga (O'Dugan), the race of *Gaileng*, and they
gave name to the barony of Gallen in Mayo.

Gallon is used in Cavan to signify a measure of land.

Gallow; another form of Gallagh, which see.

Gardrum, Gargrim ; *Gearr-dhruim*, short ridge or hill :
d changed to *g* in Gargrim (see p. 4).

Garnavilla in Tipperary ; *Garran-a'-bhile* [Garranavilla],
the shrubbery of the *bilĕ* or old tree.

Garracloon ; *Garbh-chluain*, rough meadow.

Garran, Garrane, Garraun ; *Garrán*, a shrubbery.

Garranamanagh ; the shrubbery of the monks (*manach*).

Garranbane, Garranbaun; white shrubbery.

Garranekinnefeake ; Kinnefeake's shrubbery.

Garry; a garden (*garrdha*).

Garryard; high garden.

Garrycastle. The Mac Coghlans' castle, near Banagher
in King's County, is called in the annals *Garrdha-an-
chaislein* [Garrancashlane], the garden of the castle;
and from this the modern name Garrycastle has been
formed, and extended to the barony.

Garryduff; black garden (*dubh*).

Garrymore; great garden.

Garryowen near Limerick ; Owen's garden.

Garrysallagh ; dirty garden (*salach*).

Garryspellane ; Spellane's garden.

Gartan; a little garden. See Gort in Vocabulary.

Garvagh ; *Garbhach*, rough land (from *garbh*, rough).

Garvaghy ; rough *achadh* or field.

Garvary; *Garbhaire*, rough land.

Gay island in Fermanagh; goose island (*gedh*).

Geara, Gearagh, Gairha; *Gaertha* [gairha] a bushy place along a river.

Gearhameen river at Killarney; *min* smooth, small; a *gearha* composed of small delicate bushes.

Giants' Causeway. Irish name *Clochán-na-bhFomharaigh* [Clohanavowry], the *cloghan* or stepping stones of the Fomorians. These sea rovers were magnified into giants in popular legend, and the name came to be translated "Giants' Causeway."

Girley in Meath; *Greallach* [Grallagh], a miry place.

Glack; *Glaic*, a hollow.

Glanbehy; birchy glen (*beith*).

Glantane, Glantaun; little glen.

Glanworth in Cork; recently corrupted from its Irish name, *Gleann-amhnach* [Glenounagh], as it is written in the Book of Rights, the watery or marshy glen.

Glascloon; green *cloon* or meadow.

Glasdrummon, Glasdrummond; green ridge.

Glashaboy, Glashawee; yellow streamlet (*glaise* and *buidhe*).

Glasheen; a little stream.

Glasmullagh; green *mullach* or summit.

Glasnevin near Dublin; takes name from a streamlet flowing through Delville into the Tolka at the bridge. In remote ages some pagan chief named *Naeidhe* [Nee], must have resided on its banks; from him it was called *Glas-Naeidhen* [Neean], F. M., *Naeidhe's* streamlet; and the name extended to the village, while its original application is quite forgotten.

Glassan; a green place.

Glasthule; *Glas-Tuathail* [thoohil], *Tuathal's* or Toole's streamlet.

Glenagarey; *Gleann-na-gcaerach* [Glenagaira], the glen of the sheep (*caera*).

Glenanair; the glen of slaughter (*ár*).

Glenavy in Antrim. The *G* is a modern addition. The Irish name, as given in the Calendar, is *Lann-Abhaich* [Lanavy], the church of the dwarf. When St. Patrick had built the church there, he left it in charge of his disciple Daniel, who, from his low stature, was called *Abhac* [avak or ouk], i. e. dwarf.

Glenbane, Glenbaun; white glen.

Glencar on the borders of Leitrim and Sligo; *Gleann-a'-chairthe* [Glenacarha], the glen of the pillar stone (*cairthe*).

Glencullen, Glencullin; holly glen (*cuillionn*).

Glendine, Glandine; deep glen (*doimhin*).

Glendowan mountains in Donegal; same as Glendine.

Glenduff; black glen (*dubh*).

Glengarriff; rough or rugged glen (*garbh*).

Gleninagh; ivy glen (see *eidhneán* in Vocabulary).

Glenkeen; beautiful glen.

Glenmore; great glen.

Glennamaddy; the valley of the dogs (*madadh*).

Glenogra in Limerick; Ogra's glen.

Glenosheen in Limerick; *Oisin's* or Osheen's glen.

Glenquin, barony of, in Limerick; see p. 4.

Glenreagh, Glenrevagh; grey glen.

Glenroe; red glen (*ruadh*).

Glentane, Glentaun; little glen.

Glenties in Donegal; *Gleanntaidhe* [glenty], glens; from two fine glens at the head of which it stands.

Glenwhirry in Antrim; *Gleann-a'-choire* [Glenacurry: change of *ch* to *wh*), the glen of the river Curry or *Coirĕ*. *Coirĕ* means a caldron, and the river got this name from a deep pool formed under a cataract.

Glynn; a glen or valley.

Gneeve, Gneeves; *Gniomh* [gneeve], a measure of land.

Gola; forks; the plural of *gabhal* [goul].

Golan; a little *goul* or fork.

Golden in Tipperary; *Gabhailin* [Gouleen], a little fork: the Suir divides there for a short distance, forming a fork.

Gort; *Gort*, a tilled field.

Gortahork, Gortahurk; the field of the oats (*coirce*).

Gortalassa; the field of the *lis* or fort.

Gortanure, Gortinure; the field of the yew.

Gortavoher; the field of the *boher* or road.

Gortboy; yellow field (*buidhe*).

Gortbrack; speckled field (*breac*).

Gorteen ; little field.

Gortfad, Gortfadda ; long field.

Gortgranagh ; grain field.

Gortin ; little field ; same as Gorteen.

Gortmore ; great field.

Gortnaglogh ; *Gort-na-gcloch,* the field of the stones.

Gortnagross ; *Gort-na-gcros,* the field of the crosses.

Gortnahoo, Gortnahoon ; the field of the cave (*uaimh*).

Gortnamona ; the field of the bog (*moin*).

Gortnamucklagh ; the field of the piggeries.   See Mucklagh.

Gortnasillagh ; the field of the sallows.

Gortnaskea, Gortnaskeagh, Gortnaskeha, Gortnaskey ;
the field of the *sceachs* or whitethorn bushes.

Gortreagh ; grey field (*riabhach*).

Gortroe ; red field (*ruadh*).

Gougane Barra in Cork ; St. Finbar's rock-cleft.

Goul, Gowel ; *Gabhal,* a fork.

Gowlan, Gowlane, Gowlaun ; little fork.

Graffa, Graffin, Graffoge, Graffy ; grubbed land, or land
rooted up by a *grafaun* or grubbing axe.

Graigue ; a village.

Graiguenamanagh ; the village of the monks.

Grallagh ; *Greallach* [Grallagh], a miry place.

Granagh, Granaghan ; a place producing grain.

Grangegeeth ; windy grange (*gaeth*).

Gransha ; a grange, a place for grain.

Greagh ; a moory level spot among hills.

Great Connell ; great *congbhail* or habitation (see Con.
wal).

Greenan, Greenane, Greenaun, Grenan ; *Grianan,* a
summer residence, a royal palace.   From *grian*, the
sun.

Greenoge ; a sunny little spot.   From *grian.*

Grillagh, Grellagh ; same as Grallagh.

Gurteen ; little tilled field ; same as Gorteen.

Gurteenroe ; red little field.

Guilcagh ; a place producing broom (*giolcach,* broom).

Gyleen near Trabolgan in Cork ; little *gobhal* or fork

Heagles near Ballymoney ; *Eaglais,* a church.

Howth ; from the Danish *Hoved,* a head.   Old Irish

name *Ben Edar*, the peak of Edar, a legendary personage.

Idrone, baronies of, in Carlow. So called from the tribe of *Hy Drona* (Book of R.), the former occupants, who were named from their ancestor *Drona*, fourth in descent from Cahirmore, monarch of Ireland from A. D. 120 to 123.

Illan, Illane, Illaun; *Oileán* [oilaun], an island.

Imaile in Wicklow; *Hy Mail* (O'Dugan), the descendants of Mann *Mal*, brother of Cahirmore. See Idrone.

Inch; *Inis*, an island; a low meadow along a river.

Inchmore; great island or river meadow.

Inis, Inish; an island.

Inishannon in Cork; written in the Book of Leinster *Inis-Eoganain* [Inishowenan], Owenan's or little Owen's island or river meadow.

Inishargy in Down; called in the Taxation of 1306, *Inyscargi*, showing that the Irish form is *Inis-carraige*, the island of the rock. The rising ground where the church stands was formerly surrounded by marshes.

Inishbofin; the island of the white cow (*bo*):—name explained by a legend.

Inishkeen; beautiful island.

Inishkeeragh; the island of sheep (*caera*).

Inishlounaght in Tipperary; *Inis-leamhnachta* [lounaghta], the island or river holm of the new milk · probably because it was good grazing land.

Inishmaan, Inishmean; middle island (*meadhon*).

Inishmacsaint, a parish in Fermanagh, taking its name from an island in Lough Erne, which is called in the annals *Inis-muighe-samh* [moy-sauv], the island of the plain of sorrel, from which the present name has been formed by a corrupt pronunciation.

Inishmore; great island.

Inishowen in Donegal; the island of Owen, son of Niall of the Nine Hostages (king from 379 to 405). See Tyrone.

Inishrush; the island of the peninsula (*ros*).

Inishturk in Mayo; *Inis-tuirc*, Hy F., the boar's island (*torc*). Several islands of this name.

Inishtioge in Kilkenny; written in the Book of Leinster *Inis-Teoc, Teoc's* island.

Innisfallen in the lower Lake of Killarney; called in the Book of Leinster *Inis-Faithlenn* [Fahlen], the island of *Faithlenn*, a man's name.

Inver; *Inbhear* [inver], the mouth of a river.

Ireland's Eye. Original name *Inis-Ereann* [Eran] (the island of *Eire* or Eria, a woman), of which the present name is an attempted translation. *Eye* is the Danish *ey*, an island; and the translators understanding *Ereann* to mean Ireland, rendered the name Ireland's *Ey* (or island) instead of Eria's *Ey*. (See Origin and History of Irish Names of Places; pp. 76, 101, 104.)

Isertkelly in Galway; corrupted (similarly to the next two names) from *Diseart-Cheallaigh* [Disertkelly], F. M., *Cellach's* or Kelly's hermitage.

Isertkieran in Tipperary; the *desert* or hermitage of St. Kieran of Ossory. See Seirkieran.

Ishartmon in Wexford; the *desert* or hermitage of St. Munna. See Taghmon.

Island Magee; the island or peninsula of the *Mac Aedhas* or Magees, its former possessors. Anciently called *Rinn-Seimhne* [Rinn-sevne], the point of *Seimhne*, the old territory in which it was situated.

Iveleary in Cork; took its name from the O'Learys, its ancient proprietors. See next name.

Iverk in Kilkenny; *Ui-Eirc* [Ee-erc], O'Dugan, a tribe name, signifying the descendants of *Erc. Ui* [ee] or *uibh* [iv], signifies descendants.

Iveruss in Limerick; the old tribe of *Uibh-Rosa* the descendants of *Rosa.*

Kanturk in Cork; *Ceann-tuirc* [Kanturk], F. M., the boar's head or hill; from the hill near the town.

Keadew, Keady; *Ceide* [Keady], a hill level and smooth at top.

Keale, Keel; *Caol*, narrow; a narrow place, valley, or river.

Keeloge, Keeloges; *Caelóg*, a narrow stripe or ridge.

Keelty; *Coillte* [Coiltha], woods, from *coill.*

Keenagh, Keenaghan; a mossy place (*caenach*, moss).

Keenaght barony in Londonderry. The descendants of
Cian [Kean], son of Olioll Olum (see Connello), were
called *Cianachta* [Keenaghta], i. e. the race of *Cian.*
The O'Conors of Glengiven, who were a portion of
this tribe, possessed the barony of Keenaght, and
gave it its name.

Keimaneigh, pass of, in Cork; *Ceim-an-fhiaigh* [Kame-
an-ee], the pass of the deer (*fiadh*).

Kenmare; *Ceann-mara*, the head of the sea (*muir*), i. e.
the highest point reached by the tide in a river. See
Kinvarra and Kinsale.

Kerry. The descendants of *Ciar* [Keer: see Conne-
mara] were called *Ciarraidhe* [Keery: Book of R.],
i. e. the race of *Ciar;* they possessed the territory
lying west of Abbeyfeale, which was called from them
Ciarraighe, and ultimately gave name to the whole
county.

Kesh in Fermanagh; *Ceis* [Kesh], a wickerwork causeway.

Keshcarrigan in Leitrim; the wickerwork causeway of
the little rock.

Kilbaha; *Coill-beithe*, birch wood.

Kilbarron in Donegal; St. Barron's church.

Kilbarry in Waterford and Cork; from St. Finbar.
See Cork and Gougane Barra.

Kilbeg; small church or wood.

Kilbeggan; Beccan's church.

Kilbeheny; *Coill-beithne* [Kilbehena], F. M., birch
wood.

Kilbreedy; *Cill-Bhrighde*, St. Brigid's church.

Kilbride; the same as Kilbreedy.

Kilbroney; church of *Bronagh*, a virgin saint.

Kilcarragh in Kerry and Waterford; the church of St.
Carthach [Caurha] of Lismore.

Kilcavan in Wexford; church dedicated to St. Kevin of
Glendalough.

Kilcleagh and Kilclay; same as next name.

Kilclief in Down; *Cill-cleithe* [Kilcleha], the hurdle
church (*cliath*). The original church was constructed
of hurdles, after the early Irish fashion.

Kilcolman; St. Colman's church.

Kilcommon; St. Coman's church.

Kilcullen; *Cill-cuillinn*, the church of the holly.

Kildalkey in Meath; written in an Irish charter in the Book of Kells, *Cill-Delga*, Delga's church.

Kildare. According to Animosus, St. Brigid built her little cell here under a very high oak tree; and hence it was called *Cill-dara*, which the same writer translates *Cella quercûs*, the cell or church of the oak.

Kildimo in Limerick; St. Dima's church.

Kildorrery in Cork; *Cill-dairbhre* [Kildarrery], the church of the oaks. See Darraragh.

Kildrought in Kildare. See Celbridge.

Kilduff; black church or wood.

Kilfinnane in Limerick; the church of St. Finan. See Ardfinnan.

Kilfithmone in Tipperary; the church of the wood of the bog (*fidh* and *móin*).

Kilflyn; Flann's church.

Kilgarriff, Kilgarve; rough wood.

Kilgarvan; *St. Garbhan's* or Garvan's church.

Kilkee in Clare; St. *Caeidhe's* [Kee's] church.

Kilkeedy in Clare and Limerick; St. *Caeide's* [Keedy's] church.

Kilkeel; narrow church.

Kilkenny; *Cill-Chainnigh* [Kilkenny], F.M., the church of St. *Cainneach*, or Canice, who died in the year 598. See Aghaboe.

Killadysart; the church of the *desert* or hermitage

Killaloe in Clare and Kilkenny; *Cill-Dalua* [Killaloo. *d* aspirated—see p. 2], the church of St. Dalua or Molua, who flourished in the sixth century.

Killanummery in Leitrim; *Cill-an-iomaire* [ummera], F.M., the church of the ridge.

Killarney; *Cill-airne*, the church of the sloes.

Killashandra. The original church was built within the enclosure of a rath or fort which still partly exists; hence *Cill-a'-sean-ratha* [Killashanraha], the church of the old rath.

Killashee in Kildare; *Cill-ausaille*, the church of St. *Ausaille* or Auxilius, a contemporary of St. Patrick. Killashee in Longford is probably the church of the *sidh* or fairy hill.

Killaspugbrone near Sligo. In the Book of Armagh it
is stated that St. Patrick built a church at *Cassel
Irra* for his disciple *Brón* or Bronus, who became
bishop of *Cuil Irra*, the peninsula lying south-west
of Sligo: hence the place was called *Cill-easpuig-
Bróin*, F. M., the church of bishop Bronus (*easpug*, a
bishop).

Killaspuglonane in Clare ; *Cill-easpuig-Fhlannáin*,
F. M., the church of bishop Flannan.

Killawillin in Cork; *Cill-a'-mhuilinn*, the church of the
mill.

Killeany in Clare and Galway; the church of St. Eany
or Endeus of Aran, who flourished in the fifth century.

Killeedy in Limerick ; the church of the virgin saint
Itá or *Idĕ*, who founded a nunnery here in the early
part of the sixth century. See Kilmeedy.

Killeen, the name of more than 80 townlands; nearly
all from *Cillin* a little church; but a few from *Coillin*,
a little wood.

Killeentierna in Kerry; *Tighernach's* [Tierna's] little
church.

Killeigh in King's County ; *Cill-achaidh* [Killahy],
F. M., the church of the field.

Killenaule in Tipperary ; the church of St. *Naile*
[Nawly] or Natalis.

Killery harbour in Connemara ; corrupted by a change
of *l* to *r* (see p. 3), from *Cael-shaile* [Keelhaly], narrow sea-inlet; but the full name is *Cael-shaile-
ruadh*, F. M., the reddish (*ruadh*) narrow sea-inlet.

Killevy or Killeavy in Armagh; called, from its proxi-
mity to Slieve Gullion, *Cill-shleibhe* [Killeva], F. M.,
the church of the *sliabh* or mountain.

Killiney in Dublin ; corrupted from *Cill-inghen* [Kil-
lineen]; full name *Cill-inghen-Leinin*, the church of
the daughters of *Leinin*.

Killiney in Kerry; the same as Killeany.

Killisk, Killiskey; the church of the water (*uisge*).

Killoe; *Cill-eó*, O'C. Cal., the church of the yews

Killure; *Cill-iubhair*, the church of the yew.

Killursa; *Cill-Fhursa*, the church of St. Fursa, who
flourished in the sixth century.

Killybegs; *Cealla-beaga*, F. M., little churches.

Killygorden in Donegal; *Coill-na-gcuiridin* [Kilnagur-ridin], F. M., the wood of the parsnips.

Killyon; the church of St. *Liadhan* [Leean] or Lie-dania, mother of St. *Ciaran* of Ossory. See Seir-kieran.

Kilmacanoge in Wicklow; the church of St. *Mochonog*, one of the primitive Irish saints.

Kilmacrenan in Donegal; see p. 3.

Kilmainham near Dublin; see p. 4.

Kilmallock in Limerick; *Cill-Mocheallog* [Kilmohelog], the church of St. *Mocheallog*, who flourished in the beginning of the seventh century.

Kilmanagh near Kilkenny; *Cill-manach* (Mart. Taml.), the church of the monks.

Kilmeedy; the church of St. *Midĕ*, or Ité; for both are the same name. See Killeedy.

Kilmihil; the church of St. Michael the Archangel.

Kilmore; there are about 80 parishes and townlands of this name, most of them signifying great church, some great wood (*cill* and *coill*).

Kilmurry; there are more than fifty places of this name, which were all so called from places dedicated to the Blessed Virgin: *Cill-Mhuire*, Mary's church.

Kilnaleck; the wood of the flag-surfaced land.

Kilnamanagh in Tipperary; *Coill-na-manach*, F. M., the wood of the monks.

Kilnamona; the church of the bog (*moin*).

Kilpatrick; St. Patrick's church.

Kilquane; *Cill-Chuain*, St. Cuan's church.

Kilroot in Antrim; *Cill-ruadh*, F. M., red church.

Kilrush; the church of the wood or peninsula.

Kilskeer in Meath; the church of the virgin saint *Scire*, who flourished in the sixth century.

Kiltenanlea in Clare; *Cill-tSenain-leith*, the church of St. Senan the hoary.

Kiltullagh in Roscommon; *Cill-tulaigh*, the church of the hill.

Kiltybegs; *Coillte-beaga*, little woods.

Kilwatermoy in Waterford; *water* is here a corruption of *uachtar*, upper: the church of the upper plain.

Kinalea, barony of, in Cork; *Cinel-Aedha* [Kinel-Ay], O'Dugan, the descendants of *Aedh* or Hugh, who was the father of *Failbhe-Flann*, king of Munster in A. D. 636.

Kinalmeaky, barony of, in Cork; *Cinel-mBece* [Kinel-mecka], O'Dugan, the descendants of *Bece*, the ancestor of the O'Mahonys.

Kinard; *Ceann-ard*, high head or hill.

Kinawley in Fermanagh; *Cill-Naile* [Kilnawly, which would have been the correct anglicised form], O'C. Cal., the church of St. *Naile* or Natalis, who died in A. D. 564.

Kincon; the hound's head (*ceann* and *cu*).

Kincora at Killaloe, the site of Brian Boru's palace, took its name from an ancient weir across the Shannon; *Ceann-coradh* [Kancora], F. M., the head or hill of the weir.

Kinneigh, Kinnea; *Ceann-ech*, F. M., the horse's head or hill.

Kinnitty in King's County; *Ceann-Eitigh* [Kan-Etty], *Etech's* head; so called, according to a gloss in the Felire of Aengus, because the head of *Etech*, an ancient Irish princess, was buried there.

Kinsale, Kinsaley; *Ceann-saile*, the head of the brine, i. e. the highest point to which the tide rises in a river. See Kenmare.

Kinure; *Ceann-iubhair*, the head of the yew.

Kinvarra in Galway; *Ceann-mhara*, F. M., the head of the sea. See Kenmare.

Knappagh; *Cnapach*, a place full of *cnaps* or round hillocks.

Knock; *Cnoc*, a hill.

Knockacullen; the hill of the holly.

Knockaderry; the hill of the oak wood.

Knockagh; *Cnocach*, a hilly place.

Knockainy in Limerick; the hill of *Aine* or Ainy, a celebrated *banshee*.

Knockalisheen; the hill of the little *lis* or fort.

Knockalough; the hill of the lake.

Knockane, Knockaun; little hill.

Knockanglass, Knockaneglass; green little hill.

Knockanree ; see page 2.

Knockanroe, Knockaneroe, Knockaunroe; red little hill.

Knockanure; *Cnoc-an-iubhair*, yew hill.

Knockatemple; the hill of the temple or church.

Knockatarriv, Knockatarry, Knockaterriff; *Cnoc-a'-tairbh*, the hill of the bull.

Knockatober; the hill of the well.

Knockatoor; the hill of the *tuar* or bleach green.

Knockatotaun; *Cnoc-a'-teotain*, the hill of the burning or conflagration.

Knockaunbaun; white little hill.

Knockavilla, Knockaville; the hill of the *bilĕ* or old tree.

Knockavoe near Strabane; *Cnoc-Buidhbh* [Knockboov], F. M., the hill of Bove Derg, a legendary Tuatha De Danann chief.

Knockbane, Knockbaun; white hill.

Knockboy; *Cnoc-buidhe*, yellow hill.

Knockbrack; *Cnoc-breac*, speckled hill.

Knockcroghery in Roscommon; the hill of the *crochaire* or hangman : it was a place of execution.

Knockdoo, Knockduff; see page 2.

Knockeen; little hill.

Knockfierna in Limerick; *Cnoc-firinne*, the hill of truth, or of truthful prediction; for it serves as a *weather glass* to the people of the circumjacent plains, who can predict whether the day will be wet or dry by the appearance of the summit in the morning.

Knockglass ; *Cnoc-glas*, green hill.

Knockgorm ; *Cnoc-gorm*, blue hill.

Knocklayd in Antrim ; called from its shape *Cnoc-leithid* [lehid], the hill of breadth, i. e. broad hill.

Knocklofty in Tipperary; *Cnoc-lochta*, the *lofted* or shelving hill.

Knocklong in Limerick; *Cnoc-luinge*, the hill of the encampment; for Cormac mac Art encamped with his army, on this hill, when he invaded Munster in the third century.

Knockmanagh; middle hill.

Knockmealdown mountains; *Cnoc-Maeldomhnaigh*, Mael-downey's hill.

Knockmore; great hill.

Knockmoyle; *Cnoc-mael,* bald or bare hill.

Knockmullin; the hill of the mill.

Knocknaboley, Knocknabooly; the hill of the *booley* or dairy place.

Knocknacrohy; *Cnoc-na-croiche,* the hill of the gallows; a place of execution.

Knocknagapple, Knocknagappul; *Cnoc na-gcapall,* the hill of the horses.

Knocknagaul in Limerick; the hill of the *Galls* or foreigners.

Knocknageeha; the hill of the wind (*gaeth*).

Knocknagin; *Cnoc-na-gceann* [na-gan], the hill of the heads; a place of execution.

Knocknaglogh; the hill of the stones (*cloch*).

Knocknagore; the hill of the goats (*gabhar*).

Knocknahorna; the hill of the barley (*eórna*).

Knocknamona; the hill of the bog.

Knocknamuck; the hill of the pigs.

Knocknarea in Sligo; the hill of the executions. See Ardnarea.

Knocknaskagh, Knocknaskeagh; the hill of the *sceachs* or white thorn bushes.

Knockninny, a hill in Fermanagh, which gives name to a barony; *Cnoc-Ninnidh* [Ninny], the hill of St. *Ninnidh,* who was a contemporary of St. Columba.

Knockpatrick; Patrick's hill.

Knockraha, Knockrath, Knocknaraha; the hill of the *rath* or fort.

Knockranny; *Cnoc-raithnigh* [rahnee], ferny hill.

Knockrawer, Knockramer, Knockrower, Knockrour; *Cnoc-reamhar* [rawer or rower], *fat* or thick hill.

Knockreagh; grey hill.

Knockroe ; red hill.

Knockshanbally ; the hill of the old town.

Knocksouna near Kilmallock in Limerick; written in the Book of Lismore, *Cnoc-Samhna* [Souna], the hill of *Samhuin* [Sowan or Savin], the first of November, which was kept as a festival by the pagan Irish. See Origin and History of Irish Names of Places, p. 194.

Knocktemple; the hill of the temple or church.

Knocktopher in Kilkenny; see page 4.

Knoppoge, Knappoge; a little hill.　See Knappagh.

Kyle; about half the names partly or wholly formed from Kyle, are from *Cill,* a church; the other half from *Coill,* a wood.

Kylebeg; small church or wood.

Kylemore; generally great wood (*coill*); sometimes great church (*cill*).　Kylemore (lake) near the Twelve Pins in Connemara, is *Coill-mhor,* great wood.

Labba, Labby; *Leaba* [labba], a bed, a grave.

Labbasheeda in Clare; *Leaba-Sioda, Sioda's* or Sheedy's *labba,* bed, or grave.

Labbamolaga; St. Molaga's grave.　See Templemolaga.

Lack; *leac* [lack], a stone, a flag stone.

Lacka; the side of a hill.

Lackabane, Lackabaun; white hill side.

Lackagh; a place full of stones or flags.

Lackamore; great hill side.

Lackan; the same as Lacka: a hill side.

Lackandarragh, Lackendarragh; the hill side of the oaks.

Lackareagh; grey hill side (*riabhach*).

Lackaroe; red hill side (*ruadh*).

Lackeen; a little rock or flag.

Lacken; the same as Lacka; a hill side.

Lag, Legg; a hollow; a hollow in a hill.

Lagan; a little hollow; sometimes it means a pillar stone (*liagan*).　The river Lagan probably took its name from a little hollow on some part of its course.

Laghil, Laghile; *Leamhchoill* [Lavwhill], elm wood.

Laght; *Leacht,* a sepulchre or monument.

Laghy; a slough, a miry place.

Laharan; *Leath-fhearann* [Laharan], half land.

Lahard; *Leath-ard,* half height; a gentle hill.

Lahardan, Lahardane, Lahardaun; a gentle hill.

Lakyle; *Leath-choill,* half wood.

Lambay island near Dublin; the latter part is Danish: Lamb-ey, i. e. lamb island.　Its ancient Irish name was *Rechru* or *Reachra*; and the adjacent parish on the mainland was called from it, *Port-Reachrann* ⌈Portrahern⌉, the *port* or landing place of *Reachra,*

which in the course of ages, has been softened down
to the present name, Portraine.

Laragh, Lauragh; *Lathrach*, the site of any thing.

Laraghbryan in Kildare; Bryan's house site.

Largan; *Leargan*, the side or slope of a hill.

Largy; *Leargaidh*, same meaning as last.

Larne in Antrim; *Latharna* (Laharna: Book of L.),
the district of *Lathair* [Laher], son of Hugony the
great, monarch of Ireland before the Christian era.
Until recently it was the name of a district which
extended northwards towards Glenarm; and the town
was then called *Inver-an-Laharna,* the river mouth of
(the territory of) Larne, from its situation at the mouth
of the *Ollarbha* or Larne Water.

Latt; the same word as Laght.

Latteragh in Tipperary; *Leatracha* [Latraha], the plural
of *Leitir,* a wet hill-side (see Letter).   It is called in
O'C. Cal., *Letracha-Odhrain* [Oran], *Odhran's* wet
hill-slopes, from the patron, St. *Odhran,* who died in
the year 548.

Laughil; *Leamhchoill* [Lavwhill], elm wood.

Laune river at Killarney; *Leamhain,* F. M., elm; the
elm-producing river.

Lavagh; *Leamhach* [Lavagh], a place producing elms.

Lavally; *Leath-bhaile,* half town or townland.

Lavey in Cavan; the same as Lavagh.

Leagh; *Liath* [Leea], grey; a grey place.

Leam; *Leim,* a leap.

Leamlara in Cork; the mare's leap.

Leamnamoyle in Fermanagh; the leap of the *mael* or
hornless cow.

Lear; the same as Lyre.

Lecale, barony of, in Down; *Leth-Chathail* [Lecahil],
F. M., *Cathal's* half.   *Cathal* was a chief who flourished about the year 700, and in a division of territory, this district was assigned to him, and took his
name.

Lecarrow; *Leth-ceathramhadh* [Lecarhoo], half quarter
(of land).

Leck; the same as Lack.

Leckan, Leckaun; the same as Lackan.

Leckpatrick ; Patrick's flag-stone.

Leeg, Leek, Leeke; the same as Lack.

Legacurry, Legaghory ; *Lag-a-choire* [curry], the hollow (*lag*) of the caldron or pit.

Legan, Legaun; the same as Lagan.

Legland; same as Leighlin.   *D* added : see p. 4.

Lehinch ; *Leith-innse*, F. M., half island, i. e. a peninsula.

Leighlin in Carlow ; *Leith-ghlionn* [Leh-lin], F. M., half glen ; from some peculiarity of formation in the little river bed.

Leighmoney ; grey *muine* or shrubbery.

Leinster.   In the third century before the Christian era, *Labhradh Loingseach* [Lavra Linshagh, Lavra the mariner], brought an army of Gauls from France to assist him in recovering the kingdom from his uncle, the usurper, Coffagh Cael Bra.   These foreign soldiers used a kind of broad pointed spear, called *laighen* [layen] ; and from this circumstance the province in which they settled, which had previously borne the name of *Galian*, was afterwards called *Laighen*, which is its present Irish name.   The termination *ster*, which has been added to the names of three of the provinces, is the Scandinavian or Danish *stadr*, a place.   *Laighenster* (the place or province of *Laighen*) would be pronounced *Laynster*, which is the very name given in a state paper of 1515, and which naturally settled into the present form, Leinster.

Leitrim, the name of more than 40 townlands and villages ; *Liath-dhruim* [Lee-drum], F. M., grey *drum* or ridge.

Leixlip ; a Danish name, meaning salmon leap (*lax*, a salmon), from the well-known cataract on the Liffey, still called Salmon leap, a little above the village. By Irish-Latin writers it is often called *Saltussalmonis* (the leap of the salmon); and from this word *saltus*, a leap, the baronies of Salt in Kildare have taken their name.

Lemanaghan in King's County ; *Liath-Manchain*, F. M., St. Manchan's grey land.

Lena, Leny ; a wet meadow.

Lenamore; great wet meadow.

Lerrig in Kerry; a hill side. See Largan.

Letter; *Leitir*, a wet hill side.

Lettera, Letteragh, Lettery; wet hill-sides. See Latteragh.

Letterkenny; a shortened form of *Letter-Cannanan*, the O'Cannanans' hill-slope. The O'Cannanans, or as they now call themselves, Cannons, were anciently chiefs or kings of Tirconnell, till they ultimately sank under the power of the O'Donnells.

Lettermacaward in Donegal; *Leitir-Mic-a'-bhaird*, the hill slope of Mac Ward, or the bard's son.

Lettermore; great wet hill-side.

Lettermullan; *Leitir-Meallain*, F. M., Meallan's hill-slope.

Levally; the same as Lavally.

Leyny. The descendants of *Luigh* or Lewy, the son of *Cormac Gaileng* (see Gallen), were called *Luighne* [Leyny: O'Dugan], and they gave name to the barony of Leyny in Sligo (*ne*, descendants).

Lick; the same as Lack and Leck.

Lickbla in Westmeath; shortened from *Liag-Bladhma* [Leeg-Blawma], F. M., the flag-stone of *Bladh* [Blaw], a man's name. See Slieve Bloom.

Lickeen; little flag-stone.

Lickfinn in Tipperary; white flag-stone.

Lickmolassy in Galway; St. *Molaise's* [Molasha's] flag-stone.

Lickoran; the flag of the cold spring (*uaran*).

Limerick; corrupted from the Irish form *Luimnech* [Liminagh], F. M., by a change of *n* to *r* (see p. 3): the name signifies a bare spot of land, from *lom*, bare.

Lis, Liss; *Lios*, a circular earthen fort.

Lisalbanagh; the *Albanagh's* or Scotchman's fort.

Lisanisk, Lisanisky; the fort of the water (*uisge*).

Lisbane, Lisbaun; white *lis* or fort.

Lisbellaw; *Lios-bel-atha*, the *lis* of the ford-mouth.

Lisboy; yellow fort; probably from furze blossoms.

Liscannor in Clare; Canar's fort.

Liscarroll in Cork; *Cearbhall's* or Carroll's fort.

Liscartan; the fort of the forge (*ceardcha*).

Lisdoonvarna in Clare; takes its name from a large fort on the right of the road as you go from Ballyvaghan to Ennistymon. The proper name of this is *Dunbhearnach* [Doonvarna], gapped fort (see Barna), from its shape; and the word *Lis* was added, somewhat in the same manner as "river" in the expression "the river Liffey:" Lisdoonvarna, i. e. the *lis* (of) Doonvarna.

Lisdowney in Kilkenny; Downey's fort.

Lisduff, Lisdoo; *Lios-dubh*, black fort.

Lisheen; little *lis* or fort.

Lislea; *Lios-liath* [lee], grey fort.

Lislevane in Cork; *Lios-leamhain*, elm fort.

Lismore; great fort. Lismore in Waterford received its name from the *lis* or entrenchment built by St. *Carthach* [Caurhagh] round his religious establishment. It was previously called *Magh-sciath* [Maskee], the plain of the shield. See Origin and History of Irish Names of Places, p. 261.

Lismoyle; *Lios-mael*, bald or dilapidated fort.

Lismullin; the fort of the mill.

Lisnagat; *Lios-na-gcat*, the fort of the (wild) cats.

Lisnageeragh; the fort of the sheep (*caera*).

Lisnalee; the fort of the calves (*laegh*). See p. 2.

Lisnamuck; the *lis* or fort of the pigs.

Lisnaskea in Fermanagh; the fort of the *sceach* or whitethorn tree. It took its name from the celebrated *Sceach-ghabhra* [Skagowra], under which the Maguire used to be inaugurated.

Lisnisk, Lisnisky; the fort of the water.

Lissan, Lissane; little *lis* or fort.

Lissaniska, Lissanisky; the fort of the water.

Lissaphuca; the fort of the *pooka* or spright.

Lissard; high fort.

Listowel; *Lios-Tuathail* [Lis-Thoohil], *Tuathal's* fort.

Lissonuffy in Roscommon; *Lios-O-nDubhthaigh* [Lisōnuffy], F. M., the fort of the O'Duffys.

Lixnaw in Kerry; *Lic-Snamha* [Snawa], F. M., the flag-stone of the swimming (*snamh*). See Drumsna.

Loughill, Loughil; *Leamhchoill* [Lavwhill], elm wood.

Londonderry. Its most ancient name, according to all
our authorities, was *Doire- Chalgaich* [Derry-Calgagh],
the derry or oak wood of *Calgach* or *Galgacus*. In
the tenth or eleventh century it began to be called
Derry- Columcille, in honour of St. Columkille, who
founded his monastery there in 546; and this name
continued to the time of James I., whose charter,
granted to a company of London merchants, imposed
the name of Londonderry.

Longfield; in almost all cases a corruption of *Leamhchoill* [Lavwhill], elm wood.

Longford; *Longphort* [Longfort], a fortress. The town
of Longford is called in the Annals Longford O'Far-
rell, from a castle of the O'Farrells, the ancient proprietors.

Loop Head in Clare; a Danish modification of Leap
Head; Irish *Leim- Chonchuillinn* [Leam-Conhullin],
F. M., *Cuchullin's* leap. For legend see Origin and
History of Irish Names of Places, p. 163.

Lorum in Carlow; *Leamh-dhruim* [Lavrum], elm ridge.

Lough; a lake; an inlet of the sea.

Loughan, Loughane, Loughaun; little lake.

Loughanreagh; grey little lake.

Loughbeg; little lake.

Lough Boderg; the lake of the red cow.

Lough Bofin; the lake of the white cow.

Loughbrickland; corrupted by changing *r* to *l*, and
adding *d* (see pp. 3 and 4), from *Loch-Bricrenn*,
F. M., the lake of *Bricriu*, a chief of the first century.

Lough Conn in Mayo; *Loch-Con*, F. M., the lake of
the hound.

Lough Corrib; the correct Irish name is *Loch Orbsen*,
F. M., which was corrupted by the attraction of the
c sound in *Loch* to *Orbsen*, and by the omission of the
syllable *sen*. *Orbsen* was another name for *Manannan
Mac Lir*, a celebrated legendary personage.

Loughcrew in Meath; *Loch-craeibhe* [creeve], the lake
of the branchy tree.

Lough Derg on the Shannon; contracted from *Loch-
Dergdherc* [Dergerk], the lake of the red eye, which
is explained by a legend.

Lough Derravara in Westmeath; *Loch-Dairbhreach* [Darravara], F. M., the lake of the oaks. See Darraragh.

Lough Erne; the lake of the *Ernai*, a tribe of people.

Lough Finn; see Finn river.

Lough Guitane near Killarney; *Loch-coiteáin* [cutthaun], the lake of the little *cot* or boat.

Lough Melvin; corrupted from *Loch-Meilghe* [Melyĕ], the lake of *Meilghe*, an ancient king of Ireland.

Lough Neagh; written in the Book of Leinster *Loch-nEchach* [nehagh], the lake of *Eochy* [Ohy], a Munster chief, who was drowned in it at the time of its eruption in the first century. The *N* is a mere grammatical inflection, and the name is often used without it; for instance, we find it spelled *Lough Eaugh* in Camden, as well as in many of the maps of the 16th and 17th centuries.

Lough Oughter in Cavan; *Loch-uachtar*, upper lake, i. e. upper as regards Lough Erne.

Loughrea in Galway; *Loch-riabhach*, grey lake.

Lug; a hollow; the same as Lag and Leg.

Lugduff mountain over Glendalough; black hollow, from a hollow at the base.

Luggelaw; the hollow of the *lagh* or hill.

Lugmore; great hollow.

Lugnaquillia, the highest mountain in Wicklow; *Lug-na-gcoilleach* [Lugnagulliagh], the hollow of the cocks, i. e. grouse.

Lumcloon; bare meadow (*lom*, bare).

Lurgan; the shin; a long hill.

Lurganboy; yellow long hill.

Lurraga; the same as Lurgan.

Lusk in Dublin; *Lusca*, a cave.

Lusmagh in King's County; the plain of herbs (*lus*, an herb).

Lynally. In the sixth century there was a forest here called the wood of Ela; and the church founded by St. Colman, about the year 590, was thence called *Lann-Ealla* (O'C. Cal.), the church of *Ela*, which has been anglicised to the present name.

Lynn; a form of *Lann*, a house or church.

Lyre; *Ladhar* [Lyre], a fork formed by rivers or glens. See Lear.

Mace; *Más* [Mauce], the thigh, a long low hill.

Mackan, Mackanagh, Macknagh, Mackney; a place producing parsnips (*meacan*, a parsnip).

Macosquin in Derry; corrupted from *Magh-Cosgrain* [Macosgran], F. M., *Cosgran's* plain.

Maghera; *Machaire*, a plain. Maghera in Down and Maghera in Derry, are both contracted from *Machaire-ratha* [Maghera-raha], the plain of the fort.

Magherabeg; little plain.

Magheraboy; yellow plain.

Magheracloone; the plain of the *cloon* or meadow.

Magheraculmoney; the plain of the back (*cul*) of the shrubbery.

Magheradrool in Down; *Machaire-eadarghabhal* [Maghera-addrool], the plain between the (river) forks (*eadar*, between; and *gabhal*). See Addergoole.

Magherahamlet in Down; the plain of the *Tamlaght* or plague monument. See Tallaght.

Magheramenagh; middle plain (*meadhonach*).

Magheramore; great plain.

Magherareagh; grey plain (*riabhach*).

Maghery; a form of Maghera, a plain.

Magunihy, barony of, in Kerry; *Magh-g Coincinne* [Magunkinny], F. M., the plain of the O'Conkins.

Mahee island in Strangford Lough; the island of St. *Mochaei* [Mohee], bishop, a disciple of St. Patrick, and the founder of Nendrum.

Maigue, a river in Limerick; called *Maigh* in the annals, i. e., the river of the plain.

Mallow in Cork; called in the Annals *Magh-Ealla* [Moyallo], the plain of the river Allo, which was anciently the name of that part of the Blackwater flowing by the town. See Duhallow.

Manulla in Mayo; *Magh-Fhionnalbha* [Mah-Innalva], Hy. F., Finalva's plain.

Massareene in Antrim; *Más-a'-rioghna* [Massareena], the queen's hill.

Maul; *Meall*, a lump, a hillock.

Maum; *Madhm* [Maum], a high mountain pass.

Maumturk; the pass of the boars (*torc*).

Maw; *Magh*, a plain.

Maynooth; *Magh-Nuadhat* [Ma-nooat], F. M., *Nuadh-at's* plain; from *Nuadhat*, king of Leinster, foster-father to Owen More king of Munster. See Bear.

Mayo; *Magh-eó* [Ma-ó], the plain of the yews. Full name *Magheó-na-Saxan*, F. M., Mayo of the Saxons, from a number of English monks settled there in the seventh century, by St. Colman, an Irish monk, after he had retired from the see of Lindisfarne.

Meelick; *Miliuc* [Meeluck], F. M., low marshy ground.

Meen; a mountain meadow.

Meenadreen; the mountain meadow of blackthorns.

Meenkeeragh; mountain meadow of the sheep.

Milleen; a little hillock. See Maul.

Moan; *Moin* [mone], a bog. See Mon.

Moanduff; black bog.

Moanmore; great bog.

Moanroe; red bog.

Moanvane, Moanvaun; *Moin-bhán*, white bog.

Moat; *Móta*, a high mound.

Moate in Westmeath; from the great mound at the village; full name Moategranoge, the moat of *Grainĕ-óg* or young Grace, who, according to tradition, was a Munster princess.

Mocollop; the plain (*magh*) of the *collops* or cattle.

Modeshill; *Magh-deisiol* [Ma-deshil], southern plain.

Mogeely; *Magh-Ilĕ*, F. M., the plain of *Ilĕ* or Ely.

Moher; see Cliffs of Moher.

Mohill; *Maethail* [Mwayhill], soft or spongy land; from *maeth*, soft.

Moig, Moigh; forms of *Magh*, a plain.

Moira; *Magh-rath*, F. M., the plain of the forts.

Mon; a bog. See Moan.

Monabraher, Monambraher, Monamraher; *Moin-na-mbrathar*, F. M., the bog of the friars.

Monagay in Limerick; the bog of the goose (*gedh*); from wild geese.

Monaghan; *Muineachán*, F. M., a place full of little hills or brakes (*muine*).

Monamintra in Waterford ; *Moin-na-mbaintreabhaigh* [Monamointree], the bog of the widows.

Monard; high bog.

Monasteranenagh in Limerick ; *Mainister-an-aenaigh* [Monasteraneany], F. M., the monastery of the fair Anciently called *Aenach-beag*, little fair.

Monasterboice in Louth; the monastery of St. *Boethius* or *Buite*, who founded it in the sixth century.

Monasterevin; the monastery of St. Evin, the founder a contemporary of St. Patrick.

Monasteroris in King's County; *Mainister-Fheorais*, [*ōrish : F* aspirated and omitted — see p. 2], the monastery of Mac *Feorais* or Bermingham, who founded it in A. D. 1325.

Monear; a meadow.

Moneen; a little bog (*moin*).

Money; *Muine* [munny], a shrubbery.

Moneydorragh; *Muine-dorcha*, dark or gloomy shrubbery.

Moneyduff; *Muine-dubh*, black shrubbery.

Moneygall; the shrubbery of the *Galls* or foreigners.

Moneygorm; *Muine-gorm*, blue shrubbery.

Moneymore; great shrubbery.

Monivea in Galway; *Muine-an-mheadha* [Money-an-va], F. M., the shrubbery of the mead, a kind of drink.

Monroe ; *Moin-ruadh*, red bog.

Montiagh, Montiaghs; *Mointeach*, a boggy place.

Morgallion. A branch of the *Gailenga* (see Gallen), settled in Leinster, and a portion of them gave name to the territory of *Mor-Gailenga* or the great *Gailenga*, now the barony of Morgallion in Meath.

Mothel, Mothell ; same as Mohill.

Mountmellick. The old anglicised name is *Montiagh-meelick*, the bogs or boggy land of the *meelick* or marsh. See Montiagh and Meelick.

Mourne mountains in Down. The ancient name was *Beanna Boirche* [Banna-Borka], F. M., the peaks of the shepherd *Boirche*, who herded on these mountains the cattle of *Ross*, king of Ulster in the third century. About the middle of the twelfth century, a tribe of the Mac Mahons from Cremorne (see Cremorne),

settled in the south of the present county of Down,
and gave their tribe name of *Mughdhorna* [Mourna],
to the barony of Mourne, and to the Mourne mountains.

Movilla in Down; *Magh-bhile* [Ma-villa], O'C. Cal., the
plain of the ancient tree.

Moville in Donegal; the same as last.

Moy; *Magh* [mah], a plain.

Moyacomb in Wicklow; *Magh-da-chon* [Moy-a-con],
F. M., the plain of the two hounds.

Moyaliff in Tipperary; *Magh-Ailbhe* [Moyalva], F. M.,
Ailbhe's or Alva's plain.

Moyard; high plain.

Moyarget; *Magh-airgid*, the plain of silver.

Moyarta in Clare; *Magh-fherta* (*fh* silent: see p. 2),
the plain of the grave.

Moycullen in Galway; the plain of holly.

Moydow in Longford; *Magh-dumha* [Moy-dooa], F. M.,
the plain of the burial mound.

Moygawnagh in Mayo; written in the Book of Lecan,
Magh-gamhnach, the plain of the milch cows.

Moyglass; green plain.

Moygoish. The descendants of *Colla Uais* (see Cremorne), were called *Ui mic Uais* [Ee-mic-Oosh]; a
portion of whom were settled in Westmeath, and gave
their name to the barony of Moygoish.

Moyle; *Mael*, a bald or bare hill.

Moylough; the plain of the lake.

Moymore; great plain.

Moynalty in Meath; *Magh-nealta* [Moynalta], the plain
of the flocks (*ealta*).

Moyne; *Maighin* [Moin], a little plain.

Moynoe in Clare; same as Mayo: the *n* is a grammatical
accident.

Moynure; the plain of the yew (*iubhar*).

Moyrus; the plain of the *ros* or peninsula.

Moys; i. e. plains; from *magh*.

Muckamore in Antrim; *Magh-comair* [Ma-cummer],
F. M., the plain of the *cummer* or confluence (of the
Six mile Water with Lough Neagh).

Muckanagh, Muckenagh; *Muiceannach*, a resort of pigs;
a place where pigs used to feed or sleep (from *muc*).

Muckelty, Mucker, Muckera, Muckery; the same as Muckanagh.

Mucklagh; *Muclach*, same as Muckanagh.

Muckinish; pig island.

Muckloon, Mucklone, Mucklin; *Muc-chluain*, pig meadow.

Muckno in Monaghan; *Mucshnamh* [Mucknauv], F. M., the swimming place (*snamh*) of the pigs; the place where pigs used to swim across the little lake.

Muckross; the peninsula of the pigs.

Muff; a corruption of *Magh*, a plain.

Muing; a sedgy place.

Mullacrew in Louth; *Mullach-craeibhe* [Mullacreeva], the summit of the spreading tree.

Mullagh; *Mullach*, a summit.

Mullaghareirk mountains near Abbeyfeale in Limerick; *Mullach-a'-radhairc* [rīrk], the summit of the prospect.

Mullaghbane; white summit.

Mullaghboy; yellow summit.

Mullaghbrack; speckled summit.

Mullaghdoo, Mullaghduff; black summit.

Mullaghglass; green summit.

Mullaghmeen; *Mullach-mín*, smooth summit.

Mullaghmore; great summit.

Mullaghroe; *Mullach-ruadh*, red summit.

Mullan, Mullaun; a little *mullach* or summit.

Mullans; little summits.

Mullen, Mullin; *Muileann* [mullen], a mill.

Mullinahone in Tipperary; *Muileann-na-huamhainn* [Mullinahooan], the mill of the cave (*uamha*); from a cave near the village through which the little river runs.

Mullinavat in Kilkenny; *Muilenn-a'-bhata*, the mill of the stick.

Mully; the same as Mullagh.

Multyfarnham in Westmeath; *Muilte-Farannain* [Multy-Farannan], Farannan's mills (*muilenn*, plural *muilte*).

Munster. Old Irish name *Mumhan* [Mooan], which,

with *ster* added (see Leinster), forms *Mughan-ster* [Moonster] or Munster.

Murragh, Murreagh ; *Murbhach* [Murvagh], a flat marshy piece of land by the sea.

Murrow of Wicklow; same as Murragh.

Muskerry. The people descended from Carbery Musc, son of Conary II. (see Corkaguiny), were called *Mus-craidhe* [Muskery: O'Dugan] ; of these there were several tribes, one of which gave name to the two baronies of Muskerry in Cork.

Myshall in Carlow; *Muigh-íseal* [Mweeshal], low plain.

Naas in Kildare, the most ancient residence of the kings of Leinster; *Nás* [Nawce], a fair or meeting place.

Nantinan in Limerick ; *Neantanán*, a place of nettles (*neanta*).

Nappan in Antrim; *Cnapán*, a little hill.

Naul in the north of Dublin; *'n-aill* [naul], the cliff. The article incorporated : see Nenagh.

Ned; *Nead* [Nad], a bird's nest.

Nenagh in Tipperary. Irish name *Aenach* [Enagh], a fair; the *N* is a contraction for the Irish definite article "an," which has become incorporated with the word:—*'n-Aenach* [Nenagh], the fair. The full name is *Aenach-Urmhumhan* [Enagh-urooan] the fair of Ormond or east Munster; and this name is still used by those speaking Irish.

Newrath; *'n-Iubhrach* [Nuragh], the yew land; by the incorporation of the article.

New Ross. Irish name *Ros-mic-Treoin* [Rosmictrone], the wood (*ros*) of the son of *Treun*.

Newry. Ancient name *Iubhar-cinn-tragha* [Yure-Kin-traw], the yew tree at the head of the strand. In after ages this was shortened to *Iubhar*, which, with the article prefixed (see Nenagh), and *y* added, became changed to the present form Newry.

Nicker in Limerick ; *Cuinicér* [Knickere], a rabbit warren (from *coinín*).

Nobber; *Obair* [obber], work, with the article incorporated (see Nenagh):—Nobber, "the work," a name applied, according to tradition, to the English castle erected there.

Nohoval in Cork and Kerry; shortened from *Nuachong-bhail* [Nuhongval], new *congbhail* or habitation. See Conwal.

Nure; the same formation and meaning as Newry.

Nurney in Kildare and Carlow; *Urnaidhe* [urny], F. M., a prayer house or oratory, with the article incorporated. See Nenagh and Urney.

Offaly, baronies of, in Kildare. The descendants of *Ros-failghe* [faly] or *Ros* of the rings, the eldest son of Cahirmore (king of Ireland from A. D. 120 to 123) were called *Hy Failghe* (O'Dugan), i. e. the descendants of *Failghe* (see Iverk); and a portion of their ancient inheritance still retains this name, in the modernized form Offaly.

Offerlane in Queen's County; a tribe name; *Ui Foir-chealláin* [Hy Forhellane], F. M., the descendants [*ui*] of *Foircheallán*.

Oghill; *Eóchaill* [Oghill], yew wood (*eó* and *coill*).

Oneilland. *Niallán*, the fourth in descent from *Colla Da Chrioch* [cree] brother of Colla Meann (see Cremorne), was the progenitor of the tribe called *Hy Niallain* (i. e. Niallan's race), F. M., and their ancient patrimony forms the two baronies of Oneilland in Armagh, which retain the name. D added; see p. 4.

Oola in Limerick and Waterford; *Ubhla* [Oola], a place of apples, an orchard (from *ubhall* or *abhall*).

Oran; *Uaran* [uran] a cold spring.

Oranmore in Galway; great cold spring.

ughterard; upper height (*uachdar*, upper).

ulart in Wexford; *abhall-ghort* [oulort], an orchard, compounded of *abhall* and *gort*.

unageeragh river flowing into the Funcheon; *Abh-na-gcaerach*, the river of the sheep.

Ovens, The, near Ballincollig in Cork; called in Irish *Uamhanna* [Oovana] i. e. the caves, from the great limestone caves near the village; and the people by a slight change of pronunciation have converted these *oovans* or caves into *ovens*. See Athnowen.

Owbeg river; *Abh-beag*, little river.

Owenass river at Mountmellick; the river of the cataract (*eas*).

Owenboy; yellow river (*abhainn*).

Owenclogy; stony river (*abhainn* and *cloch*).

Owenduff; black river.

Owenmore; *Abhainn-mór*, great river.

Owenreagh; grey river (*riabhach*).

Oxmantown or Ostmantown in Dublin; so called because the Danes or Ostmen had a fortified settlement there.

Ox mountains: called in Irish *Sliabh-ghamh* [Slievegauv], F. M., the mountain of the storms, which in the spoken language was mistaken for *Sliabh-dhamh*, the mountain of the oxen, and translated accordingly.

Park; Irish *Pairc*, a field.

Parkmore; great field.

Phœnix Park in Dublin, took its name from a beautiful spring well near the Viceregal Lodge, called *Fionnuisg'* [feenisk], clear or limpid water.

Poll; a hole, pit, or pool.

Pollacappul; *Poll-a'-chapaill*, the hole of the horse.

Pollagh; a place full of holes or pits.

Pollanass at Glendalough; the pool of the waterfall.

Pollans; holes, pools, or pits.

Pollaphuca; the *pooka's* or demon's hole.

Pollrone in Kilkenny; *Poll-Ruadhain* [Ruan], *Ruadhan's* hole.

Pollsallagh, Pollsillagh; the hole of the sallows.

Portlaw in Waterford; *Port-lagha*, the bank or landing place of the hill.

Portmarnock; St. Mernoc's bank or landing place.

Portnashangan; the *port*, bank, or landing place of the *seangans* or pismires.

Portraine; see Lambay island.

Portrush in Antrim; *Port-ruis*, the landing place of the peninsula.

Portumna in Galway; *Port-omna*, F. M., the landing place of the oak.

Pottle in Cavan; a measure of land.

Preban, Prebaun, Pribbaun; *Preabán*, a patch.

Pubble; *Pobul,* people, a congregation.

Pubblebrien in Limerick; O'Brien's people; for it was the patrimony of the O'Briens.

Pullagh; a place full of holes.

Pullans, Pullens; little holes or pits.

Quilcagh mountain at the source of the Shannon in Cavan; *Cailceach,* chalky; from its white face.

Quilly; *Coillidh* [cuilly], woodland.

Racavan; *Rath-cabhain,* the fort of the hollow.

Rahan in King's County; *Raithin,* a ferny place.

Rahaniska, Rahanisky; the rath of the water.

Rahard; *Rath-ard,* high fort.

Raharney in Westmeath; *Rath-Athairne,* Aharny's fort.

Raheen; little rath or fort.

Raheenduff; black little fort.

Raheenroe; *Raithin-ruadh,* red little fort.

Rahelty; *Rath-eilte,* the fort of the doe (*eilit*).

Raheny near Dublin; *Rath-Enna,* F. M., Enna's fort.

Rahugh in Westmeath; the fort of St. *Aedh* or Hugh, the son of *Brec,* who built a church in the old rath in the sixth century.

Raigh; same as Rath, a fort.

Rakeeragh; the fort of the sheep (*caera*).

Ramoan in Antrim; *Rath-Modhain,* Modan's fort.

Ranaghan, Rannagh; a ferny place (*raithne,* a fern).

Raphoe in Donegal; *Rath-bhoth* [Ra-voh], Γ. M., the fort of the *boths,* tents, or huts.

Rasharkin in Antrim; *Ros-Earcáin,* Erkan's promontory.

Rashee in Antrim; *Rath-sithe* [Ra-shee], F. M., the fort of the fairies.

Ratass in Kerry; *Rath-teas,* southern fort.

Rath; a circular fort.

Rathangan in Kildare; *Rath-Iomghain* [Rath-Imgan], Imgan's fort.

Rathanny; *Rath-eanaighe,* the fort of the marsh.

Rathaspick; the fort of the bishop (*easpug*).

Rathbane, Rathbaun; white rath.

Rathbeg; little fort.

Rathborney in Clare; *Rath-boirne,* the fort of Burren, from its situation in the old district of Burren.

Rathcormack; Cormac's fort.

Rathdowney in Queen's County; *Rath-tamhnaigh* [Rath-towney], F. M., the fort of the green field (*tamhn-ach*).

Rathdrum; the fort of the long hill.

Rathduff; black fort.

Rathfeigh in Meath; the fort of the exercise green. See Faha.

Rathfryland in Down; see page 4.

Rathglass; green fort.

Rathkeale; *Rath-Gaela*, Gaela's fort.

Rathkenny; *Rath-Cheannaigh* [Kanny], *Ceannach's* fort.

Rathkieran in Kilkenny; Kieran's fort; from St. Kieran of Ossory. See Seirkieran.

Rathmore; great fort.

Rathmoyle; bald or dilapidated fort.

Rathmullan; *Rath-Maelain*, F. M., Maelan's rath.

Rathnew in Wicklow; *Rath-Naoi*, F. M., *Naoi's* fort.

Rathreagh; *Rath-riabhach*, grey fort.

Rathroe; red fort.

Rathronan; Ronan's fort.

Rathsallagh; *Rath-salach*, dirty fort.

Rathvilly in Carlow; *Rath-bilĕ*, F. M., the fort of the old tree.

Rattoo; *Rath-tuaidh* [too], northern fort.

Raw; *Rath*, a fort.

Rea; *Reidh*, a coarse mountain flat.

Reask, Reisk; *Riasg* [Reesk], a marsh.

Reen; *Rinn*, a point of land.

Relagh; *Reidhleach* [Relagh], same meaning as Rea.

Relickmurry; *Reilig*, a church : the church of the Blessed Virgin Mary.

Riesk; a marsh; same as Reask.

Rin, Rine, Rinn; *Rinn*, a point of land.

Ring; another form of Rin.

Ringabella near the mouth of Cork harbour; the point of the old tree (*bilĕ*).

Ringagonagh near Dungarvan; *Rinn-O'gCuana* [Ogoo-na],the point or peninsula of the O'Cooneys.

Ringbane, Ringbaun; white point.

Ringcurran near Kinsale; the point of the *corrán* or reaping hook ; from its shape.

Ringrone near Kinsale; written in the Annals of Innisfallen, *Rinn-róin*, the point of the seal.

Ringvilla, Ringville; *Rinn-bhile* [villá], the point of the
  bilĕ or ancient tree.

Rinneen; little point of land.

Rinville in Galway; *Rinn-Mhil* [vil], the point of *Mil*,
  a Firbolg chieftain.

Risk; same as Reask.

Roeillaun; *Ruadh-oilean* [Roo-illaun], red island.

Rooaun, Rooghan, Rooghaun; reddish land (from *ruadh*,
  red).

Roosk; *Rusg*, a marsh.   See Reask.

Roosca, Rooskagh, Roosky; *Rusgach*, marshy, a marshy
  place.

Roscommon; *Ros-Comain*, F. M., Coman's wood, from
  St. *Coman*, who founded a monastery there in the
  eighth century.

Roscreá; written in the Book of Leinster, *Ros-cre*, *Cre's*
  wood.

Roshin; little *ros* or promontory.

Roskeen; *Ros-caein*, beautiful wood.

Ross; in the south generally means a wood; in the
  north, a peninsula.

Rossbegh or Rossbehy west of Killarney; the peninsula
  of birches (*beith*).

Rossbeg; small wood or promontory.

Ross Carbery in Cork; the latter part from the barony
  of Carbery in which it is situated: it was anciently called *Ros-ailithir* [allihir], F. M., the wood
  of the pilgrims.

Ross Castle at Killarney; from the little *ros* or peninsula on which it stands.

Rosses in Donegal; i. e. peninsulas.

Rossinver in Leitrim; *Ros-inbhir*, the peninsula of the
  river mouth; from a point of land running into the
  south part of Lough Melvin.

Rossmore; great wood or peninsula.

Rossorry near Enniskillen; corrupted from *Ros-airthir*
  [arher], F. M., the eastern peninsula.

Roughan, Ruan; same as Rooaun.

Rousky; same as Roosca and Rooskey.

Route. The northern part of Antrim was anciently called *Dalriada* (F. M.), i. e. *Riada's* portion or tribe, from Carbery Riada, son of Conary II. (see Corkaguiny); and the latter part (*Riada*) of this old name, is still preserved in the corrupted form of Route.

Rush in Dublin; *Ros-eo* [Rush-ō], F. M., the peninsula of the yew trees.

Rusheen; small wood; a growth of underwood.

Russagh; *Ros-each*, F. M., the wood of the horses.

Rusky; the same as Roosca and Roosky.

Saggart in Dublin; contracted from Tassagard, Irish *Teach-Sacra* [Tassacra], O'C. Cal., the house of St. *Sacra*, who flourished in the seventh century.

Saint Mullins in Carlow; Irish name *Tigh-Moling* [Tee-Molling], O'C. Cal., the house of St. *Moling*, a native of Kerry, who erected a church there about the middle of the seventh century. See Timolin.

Salt, baronies of, in Kildare; see Leixlip.

Santry in Dublin; *Sentreibh* [Shantrev; Mart. Taml.], old tribe.

Saul near Downpatrick; *Sabhall* [Saul], a barn. *Dichu*, the prince of the surrounding district, was St. Patrick's first convert in Ireland; the chief made the saint a present of his barn, to be used temporarily as a church; and hence the place was called *Sabhall-Patrick*, St. Patrick's barn, now shortened to Saul.

Scalp; *Scealp* [Scalp], a cleft or chasm.

Scarawalsh in Wexford; Irish name *Sgairbh-a'-Bhreathnaigh* [Scarriff-a-vranny], Walsh's scarriff or shallow ford (see Ballybrannagh); which, with an obvious alteration, has given name to the barony of Scarawalsh.

Scardan, Scardaun: *Scardan*, a cataract.

Scarriff; *Scairbh* [Scarriv], a rugged shallow ford.

Scart; *Scairt* [Scart], a thicket or cluster.

Scartaglin in Kerry; the thicket of the glen.

Scarteen; a little thicket or cluster.

Scartlea in Cork; *Scairt-liath*, grey thicket.

Scarva; another form of Scarriff.

Seagoe; *Suidhe-Gobha* [Seegow], the seat of St. *Gobha* [gow] or Gobanus

Seapatrick; Patrick's seat (*suidhe*).

See; *suidhe* [see], a seat or sitting place.

Seefin; *Suidhe-Finn* [Seefin], the seat of Finn Mac Coole.

Seein in Tyrone; same as Seefin, with *f* aspirated and omitted (*Suidhe-Fhinn*).

Seirkieran near Parsonstown. St. *Ciaran* or Kieran of Ossory, disciple of St. Finnian of Clonard, erected a monastery in the sixth century, at a place called *Saighir* [Sair], which was the name of a fountain; and after the saint's time it was called *Saighir-Chiarain* [Sairkeeran], now contracted to Seirkieran.

Seltan; a place of sallows.

Seskin; *Sescenn*, a marsh.

Sessia, Sessiagh; *Seiseadh* [shesha], the sixth part.

Shallon; *Sealán*, a hangman's rope, a gallows.

Shan; *Sean* [shan], old.

Shanaclogh; *Seancloch*, old stone castle.

Shanacloon; old cloon or meadow.

Shanagarry; old *garry* (*garrdha*) or garden.

Shanagolden in Limerick; *Seanguatann* [Shanagoolan], old shoulder or hill.

Shanakill; old church.

Shanavally, Shanbally; old *bally* or town.

Shanbogh, Shanbo; old *both* or tent.

Shandon; old *dun* or fortress.

Shandrum; old *drum* or ridge.

Shangarry; same as Shanagarry.

Shankill; old church.

Shanmullagh; old *mullach* or summit.

Shantallow; *Sean-talamh* [Shantalav], old land.

Shanvally; old *bally* or town (*b* aspirated).

Shean, Sheean, Sheeaun; *Sidheán* [sheeaun], a fairy hill.

Shee; *sidh* [shee], a fairy, a fairy hill.

Sheeroe; red fairy hill.

Sheetrim; *Sidh-dhruim* [Sheedrim), fairy ridge.

Shelburne barony in Wexford; from the tribe of *Siol-Brain* (O'Dugan), the seed or progeny of *Bran*.

Shelmaliere in Wexford; the descendants of Maliere or *Maelughra* [Meelura].

Sheskin; *Sescenn*, a marsh. See Seskin.

Shillelagh in Wicklow; *Siol-Elaigh* (Sheelealy: O'Dugan], the seed or descendants of *Elach.*

Shinrone in King's County; *Suidhe-an-róin* [Sheenrone], F. M., the seat of the *ron*, i. e. literally a seal, but figuratively a hirsute or hairy man.

Shrone; *srón*, a nose, a pointed hill.

Shruel, Shrule; see page 3.

Sion; *sidheán* [sheeaun], a fairy mount.

Skagh; *Sceach*, a white thorn bush.

Skahanagh, Skehanagh; a place full of *sceachs* or white thorns.

Skeagh, Skea; the same as Skagh.

Skeheen; a little *sceach* or bush.

Skelgagh; a place of *skelligs* or rocks.

Skellig rocks off the coast of Kerry; *Sceilig* means a rock.

Skerries, Skerry; *Sceir* [sker], a sea rock; *sceire* [skerry], sea rocks.

Skreen, Skrine; *Scrín* [skreen], a shrine.

Sleaty in Queen's County; *sleibhte* [Sleaty], F. M., i. e. mountains, the plural of *sliabh*: from the adjacent hills of *Slieve* Margy.

Slee; *Slighe* [slee], a road.

Slemish mountain in Antrim, on which St. Patrick passed his youth herding swine; *Sliabh-Mis*, the mountain of *Mis*, a woman's name.

Sleveen; little *slieve* or mountain.

Slieve; *Sliabh* [sleeve], a mountain.

Slieve Anierin in Leitrim; *Sliabh-an-iarainn*, the mountain of the iron; from its richness in iron ore.

Slievebane, Slievebaun; white mountain.

Slievebeagh, a range of mountains on the borders of Monaghan, Fermanagh, and Tyrone; *Sliabh-Beatha* [Slieve Baha], F. M., the mountain of *Bith*, a legendary hero.

Slieve Bernagh in the east of Clare; *Sliabh-bearnach*, gapped mountain. See Lisdoonvarna.

Slievebloom; *Sliabh-Bladhma* [Slieve-Blawma], F. M., the mountain of *Bladh* [Blaw], one of the Milesian heroes.

Slieveboy; yellow mountain.

Slieve Corragh; rugged mountain.

Slieve Donard, the highest of the Mourne mountains. *Domhanghart* [Donart], son of the king of Ulidia, and one of St. Patrick's disciples, built a little church on the very summit of this mountain; hence it was called *Sliabh-Domhanghart, Donart's* mountain, now anglicised Slieve Donard. Its ancient name was Slieve Slanga, from the bardic hero *Slaingĕ*, the son of Parthalon, who was buried on its summit, where his carn is still to be seen.

Slieve Eelim, a mountain range east of Limerick; *Sliabh-Eibhlinne* [Slieve-Evlinnĕ], Evlin's mountain.

Slieve Fuad near Newtownhamilton in Armagh; Fuad's mountain; from the Milesian hero Fuad, who was slain there.

Slieve League in Donegal; *Sliabh-liag*, the mountain of the flag-stones.

Slieve Lougher east of Castleisland in Kerry; *Sliabh-luachra*, rushy mountain.

Slieve Mish near Tralee; same as Slemish.

Slievenagriddle near Downpatrick; the mountain of the griddle; the *griddle* is a *cromlech* on the hill.

Slievenamon in Tipperary; *Sliabh-na-mban*, the mountain of the women. Full name *Sliabh-na-mban-Feimhinn* [Slievenamon-Fevin], the mountain of the women of *Feimheann*, the ancient territory surrounding it.

Slievenamuck; the mountain of the pigs.

Slievereagh; *Sliabh-riabhach*, grey mountain.

Slieveroe; red mountain.

Slievesnaght; the mountain of the snow (*sneacht*).

Sligo; named from the river: *Sligeach* [Sliggagh], F. M., shelly river (*slig*, a shell).

Sliguff; a corruption (see page 4) from *Slighe-dhubh* [Slee-duv], black road.

Slyne Head in Galway; Irish name *Ceann-leama* [Can-leama], the head of the *lyme* or leap (*leim*), which has been corrupted to the present name by changing *m* to *n*, and prefixing *s*. See Stabannon.

Solloghod in Tipperary; *Sulchoid* [sollohed], F. M., sallow wood.

Sonnagh; a mound or rampart.

Sragh, Srah; *srath* [srah], a river holm.

Srahan, Srahaun, Sraheen; little river holm.

Sroohill; see page 3.

Srough; *Srùth* [sruh], a stream.

Sroughmore; great *sruth* or stream.

Sruffaun; *Sruthán* [Sruhaun], a streamlet (p. 4).

Stabannon; corrupted from Tabannon, Bannon's house (*teach*), by prefixing *s*. See Slyne head.

Stackallen in Meath; *Teach-Collain* [Tacollan], F. M., Collan's house.

Staholmog in Meath; St. *Colmoc's* or *Mocholmoc's* house.

Stamullin in Meath; *Maelan's* house.

Stang; a measure of land.

Stillorgan in Dublin; *Tigh-Lorcain* [Teelorcan], *Lorcan's* or Laurence's house or church.

Stonecarthy in Kilkenny; first syllable a corruption of *stang*: Carthy's *stang* or measure of land.

Stonybatter in Dublin; stony road: see Batterstown and Booterstown.

Stook; *Stuaic* [stook], a pointed pinnacle.

Stookan, Stookeen; a little *stook* or pointed rock.

Stradbally; *Sradbhaile* [Sradvally], F. M., street-town; a town of one street.

Stradone, Stradowan; *Srath-doimhin* [Sradowan], deep *srath* or river holm.

Stradreagh; grey street.

Straduff; black river holm.

Straffan in Kildare; same as Sruffaun.

Straid, Strade, Sraud; *Sráid* [Sraud], a street.

Strancally near Youghal; *Sron-caillighe* [Srone-cally], the hag's nose or point.

Strangford Lough in Down; a Danish name; *strong fiord* or bay, from the well-known tidal currents at its entrance. Irish name *Loch Cuan*.

Struell; see page 3.

Sylaun; a place of sallows.

Taghadoe in Kildare; *Teach-Tuae* [Taghtoo], F. M., the house of St. Tua.

Taghboy; yellow house.

Taghmon in Wexford; written in the Book of Leinster
  Teach-Munna [Taghmunna], the house of St. Munna
  or Fintan, who founded a monastery there, and died
  in A. D. 634.

Tallaght in Dublin; *Taimhleacht* [Tavlaght], a plague
  monument. According to the bardic legend, 9000
  of Parthalon's people died of the plague, and were
  buried in this place, which was therefore called
  the *Taimhleacht* or plague grave of Parthalon's
  people.

Tamlaght, Tamlat; a plague grave; same as Tallaght.

Tamnagh, Tamny; *Tamhnach*, a green field.

Tanderagee; a corruption of *Tóin-re-gaeith* [Tonregee],
  backside to the wind. See Tonlegee.

Tara; *Teamhair* [Tawer], F. M., a residence on an
  elevated spot, commanding an extensive view. There
  are many places of this name in Ireland, besides the
  celebrated Tara in Meath.

Tarmon; the same as Termon.

Tat, Tate, Tath; a measure of land.

Tattygare; short *tate* or land measure.

Taughboyne in Donegal; *Tech-Baeithin* [Taghbwee-
  heen], O'C. Cal., the house of St. *Baeithin;* he was
  a companion of St. Columkille, and governed the
  monastery of Iona after that saint's death. Died in
  A. D. 600.

Tavanagh, Tavnagh; *Tamhnach*, a green field.

Tawlaght; a plague monument. See Tallaght.

Tawnagh, Tawny; *Tamhnach*, a green field.

Tawnaghmore; great field.

Tecolm in Queen's County; *Tigh-Choluim* [Teecolum].
  St. Columkille's house.

Teebane; *Tigh-bán* [Teebaun], white house.

Teemore; great house (*tigh*).

Teev, Teeve; *Taebh*, the side, a hill side.

Teltown on the Blackwater in Meath. Lewy of the
  long hand, one of the Tuatha De Danann kings,
  established a fair or gathering of the people, to be
  held here yearly on the first of August, in which
  games, pastimes, and marriages were celebrated; and
  in honour of his foster mother *Taillte* [Telta], he

called the place *Tailltenn* [Teltenn], now modernized to Teltown.

Temple; *Teampull,* a church.

Templeachally in Tipperary; the church of the *cala* or marshy meadow.

Templebredon in Tipperary; O'Bredon's church.

Templebreedy; St. Brigid's church.

Templecarn in Donegal; the church of the carn or monument.

Temple-etney in Tipperary; St. Eithne's church.

Templemichael; the church of the Archangel Michael.

Templemolaga in Cork; the church of St. *Molaga,* a native of Fermoy, who died on the 20th of January, some short time before the year 664.

Templemore; great church; a cathedral.

Templemoyle; bald or dilapidated church (*mael*).

Templenacarriga; the church of the rock.

Templenoe, Templenew; *Teampull-nua,* new church.

Templepatrick; St. Patrick's church.

Templeport; the church of the *port* or bank.

Templeshanbo in Wexford. Ancient pagan name *Sean-both-Sine* [Shanboh-Sheena], *Sin's* or Sheen's old tent or hut; and in Christian times, after a church had been erected there, the present name was formed by the addition of the word *Temple* to *Seanboth:* Templeshanbo, the church of *Seanboth.*

Templetogher in Galway; the church of the causeway (*tóchar*), from a celebrated old *togher* across a bog.

Templetuohy in Tipperary; the church of the *tuath* or territory, because it was the principal church of the district.

Tempo in Fermanagh; shortened from the full Irish name *an t-Iompodh-deisiol* [an Timpo deshill], the turning from left to right. *Iompodh* [impo] means turning; *deisiol,* right handed; and the article *an* prefixed takes a *t* in this case, which became incorporated with the word. The place received its name, no doubt, from the ancient custom of turning sunways in worship.

Terenure; *Tir-an-iubhair,* the land of the yew.

Termon; *Tearmann,* church land.

Termonfeckin; St. *Fechin's* church land.

Terryglass in Tipperary; called in Irish authorities *Tir-da-ghlas* [Tir-ā-glas], which Adamnan in his Life of St. Columba translates *Ager-duorum-rivorum*, the land of the two streams.

Thurles in Tipperary; *Durlios* [Durlas], strong *lis* or fort. In the annals it is commonly called Durlas-O'Fogarty, from the O'Fogartys, the ancient proprietors of the surrounding district. See Eliogarty.

Tiaquin, barony of, in Galway; shortened from *Tigh-Dachonna* [Tee-āconna], F. M., St. Dachonna's house.

Tibberaghny in Kilkenny: *Tiobrad-Fachtna* [Tibbrad-aghna], F. M., St. Faghna's well

Tibohine in Roscommon; *Tech-Baeithin* (O'Cal. Cal.), St. *Baeithin's* house. The name is the same as Taughboyne, but this is a different *Baeithin;* he was of the race of *Enda,* son of Niall of the Nine Hostages, and was one of the ecclesiastics to whom the apostolic letter was written in the year 640, on the subject of the time for celebrating Easter.

Tieve; *Taebh* [teeve], a side, a hill-side.

Tievebrack; speckled hill-side.

Tiglin in Wicklow; the house of the glen.

Tiknock, Ticknock, Ticknick; *Tigh-cnuic* [Ticknick], the house of the hill.

Timahoe in Queen's County; *Tech-Mochua* [Tee-Mohua], O'C. Cal., the house of St. *Mochua*, the original founder and patron, who flourished in the sixth century.

Timogue in Queen's County; St. Mogue's house.

Timoleague in Cork; *Teach-Molaga,* F. M., *Molaga's* house, from St. Molaga of Templemolaga.

Timolin in Kildare; *Tigh-Moling* [Tee-Moling], St. Moling's house, from a church erected there by St. Moling of St. Mullins.

Tinamuck; *Tigh-na-muc,* the house of the pigs.

Tincurragh, Tincurry; *Tigh-an-churraigh* [Tincurry], the house of the *currach* or marsh.

Tinnahinch, Tinnehinch; *Tigh-na-hinnse* [Tee-na-hinsha], the house of the island or river meadow.

Tinnakill, Tinnakilly; the house of the church or wood.

Tinnascart, Tinnascarty; the house of the cluster or thicket (*scairt*).

Tinnick, Tinnock, Tinock; same as Tiknock.

Tipper; a form of *Tobar*, a well.

Tipperary; *Tiobraid-Arann* [Tibrad-Auran], F. M., the well of *Ara*, the ancient territory in which it was situated. The well that gave this name to the town and thence to the county, was situated in the Main-street, but it is now closed up.

Tipperkevin in Kildare; St. Kevin's well.

Tipperstown in Dublin and Kildare; a half translation from *Baile-an-tobair* [Ballintubber], the town of the well.

Tiranascragh in Galway; *Tir-an-eascrach*, the land of the *esker* or sand hill.

Tirawly, barony of, in Mayo; *Tir-Amha jaidh* [Awly], the land or district of *Amhalgaidh*, king of Connaught, brother of the monarch *Dathi*, and son of Ohy Moy-vane, king of Ireland from A. D. 358 to 365.

Tirconnell, the ancient name of Donegal; *Tir-Conaill*, the land or district of Conall Gulban, son of Niall of the Nine Hostages.

Tireragh, barony of, in Sligo; *Tir-Fhiachrach* [Tir-eeragh], F. M., the district of *Fiachra*, son of *Dathi*, and grandson of Ohy Moyvane. See Tirawly.

Tirerrill, barony of, in Sligo; *Tir-Oiliolla* [ollila], Hy F., the district of Olioll, son of Ohy Moyvane (see Tirawly). *L* changed to *r*: see p. 3.

Tirkeeran, barony of, in Derry; *Tir-Chaerthainn* [Tir-keerhin], the district of Kieran, the great grandson of *Colla Uais*, brother of *Colla Meann*. See Cremorne.

Tisaran in King's County; from an old church which is called in the Calendars *Teach-Sarain* [Tasaran], the house of St. Saran, the founder, who was of the race of the *Dealbhna*. See Delvin.

Tisaxon; the house of the Saxons or Englishmen.

Tiscoffin in Kilkenny; see page 4.

Tober; *Tobar*, a well.

Toberaheena; the well of Friday (*aeine*, pron. eena); from the custom of visiting the well and performing devo-tions on Friday.

Toberbilly; the well of the ancient tree (*bilĕ*).

Tobercurry in Sligo; written by Mac Firbis, *Tober-an-choire*, the well of the caldron or pit.

Tobermore; great well.

Toberreendoney in various counties; *Tobar-righ-an-domhnaigh* [Toberreendowny], the well of the king of Sunday (i. e. of God); these wells were so called because they were visited on Sunday.

Togher; *Tóchar*, a causeway.

Tomdeely in Limerick; the tumulus (*tuaim*) of the river Deel.

Tomfinlough in Clare; *Tuaim-Fionnlocha*, F. M., the tumulus of the bright lake (*fionn*, bright, clear); from an old church by a lake near Sixmile-bridge.

Tomgraney in Clare; *Tuaim-greine* [Toomgraney], F. M., the tumulus of the lady *Grian*, about whom there are many traditions.

Tomies mountain over the lower lake of Killarney; *Tumaidhe* [Toomy], tum•li or monumental mounds; from two sepulchral heaps on the top of the mountain.

Tomregan in Cavan; *Tuaim-Drecon* [Toom-reckon: *D* aspirated—see p. 2], F. M., Drecon's burial mound.

Tonagh; *Tamhnach* [Townagh], a field.

Tonbane, Tonbaun; white *tóin* or *backside*.

Tonduff; black *backside* (*tóin*).

Tonlegee; *Tóin-le-gaeith*, *backside* to the wind.

Tonnagh; a mound or rampart.

Tonregee; same as Tanderagee and Tonlegee.

Tonroe; red backside.

Tooman; *Tuaman*, a small tumulus.

Toome, Toom; *Tuaim* [Toom], a tumulus or burial mound.

Toomore, Toomour; *Tuaim-dha-bhodhar* [Toom-ā-wour], F. M., the tumulus of the two deaf persons.

Toomyvara in Tipperary, exactly represents the sound of the Irish *Tuaim-ui-Mheadhra*, the tumulus or tomb of O'Mara.

Toor, *Tuar*, a bleach green or drying place.

Toorard; high bleach green.

Tooreen; little bleach green.

Toormore; great bleach green.

Toortane, Toortaun; *Tortan*, a small hillock.

Tor; a tower, a tall tower-like rock.

Torc mountain at Killarney; the mountain of the *torcs* or boars.

Tormore; great tower or tower-like rock.

Tory island off the coast of Donegal; *Torach* (Wars of GG.), towery, i. e. abounding in *tors* or tower-like rocks.

Touaghty in Mayo; *Tuath-Aitheachta* [Thoo-ahaghta], Hy. F., the *tuath* or district of the *attacotti* or plebeians, i. e. the races vanquished and enslaved by the Milesians.

Tourin; little bleach green; same as Tooreen.

Tralee; *Traigh-Li* [Tralee], F. M., the strand of the Lee, a little river which runs into the sea at the town, but which is now covered over.

Tramore; *Traigh-mor*, great strand.

Trean, Trien; *Trian*, a third part.

Treanbaun; white third.

Treanboy; yellow third.

Treanlaur; middle third (*lár*, middle).

Treanmanagh; middle third (*meadhonach*).

Trevet in Meath; *Trefoit* [Trefote], F. M., three *fods* or sods; so named, according to the *Leabhar-na-huidhre*, because when Art, the son of Conn of the Hundred Battles was buried there, three sods were dug over his grave in honour of the Trinity.

Trillick; *Tri-liag*, three *liags* or pillar stones.

Trim in Meath; full name *Ath-truim* [Ah-trim], the ford of the elder bushes.

Tromaun; a place producing elder bushes (*trom*).

Trough, barony of, in Monaghan; *Triucha* [Truha], a cantred or district.

Trumman, Trummery; same as Tromaun.

Tuam in Galway; *Tuaim-da-ghualann* [Tuam-a-woolan], the tumulus of the two shoulders, from the shape of the old sepulchral mound that gave name to the place.

Tubbrid; same as Tober; a well.

Tulla, Tullach; *Tulach*, a little hill.

Tullaghan; a little *tulach* or hill.

Tullaghmelan in Tipperary; Moylan's hill.

Tullahogue in Tyrone; *Tulach-og*, F. M., the hill of the youths.

Tullahaught in Kilkenny; *Tulach-ocht*, the hill of the eight (persons).

Tullamore; great hill; same as Tullymore.

Tullig; another form of *Tulach*, a hill.

Tullow; *Tulach*, a little hill.

Tullowphelim, a parish containing the town of Tullow in Carlow; contracted from Tullow-offelimy, the *tulach* or hill of the territory of the Hy Felimy, a tribe descended and named from Felimy, son of Enna Kinsella, king of Leinster in the fourth century.

Tully; a little hill; same as Tulla.

Tullyallen; *Tulaigh-áluinn* [Tullyaulin], beautiful hill.

Tullyard; high hill.

Tullybane, Tullybaun; *Tulaigh-bán*, white hill.

Tullybeg; little *tulach* or hill.

Tullycorbet; the hill of the chariot (*carbad*).

Tullyglass; green hill.

Tullyhaw, barony of, in Cavan; so called from the Magaurans, its ancient proprietors, whose tribe name was *Tealach-Echach* [Tulla-eha: O'Dugan], the family of *Eochy* or Ohy.

Tullylease in Cork; *Tulach-lias* [Tullaleese], the hill of the huts.

Tullymongan at Cavan; *Tulach-Mongain*, F. M., Mongan's hill.

Tullymore; great hill; same as Tullamore.

Tullynacross; the hill of the cross.

Tullynagardy near Newtownards; *Tulaigh-na-gceard-cha*, the hill of the forges.

Tullynaskeagh; the hill of the white thorns.

Tullynure; *Tulach-an-iubhair*, the hill of the yew.

Tullyroe; red hill.

Tullyrusk in Antrim: the hill on which the old church stands, was surrounded by marshy ground; hence the name, which Colgan writes *Tulach-ruisc*, the hill of the morass. See Rusk.

Tullytrasna; cross or transverse hill.

Tumna in Roscommon; *Tuaim-mna*, F. M., the tomb of the woman (*bean*, gen. *mna*).

Tuosist in Kerry; *Tuath-O'Siosta* [O'Sheesta], O'Siosta's territory.

Ture; the yew. The word *iubhar* [yure] has incorporated the *t* of the article, like Tempo.

Turlough; a lake that dries up in summer.

Twelve Pins, a remarkable group of mountains in Connemara; should have been called the Twelve *Bens*, i. e. peaks. Sometimes called "The Twelve Pins of Bunnabola," in which the word *beann* occurs twice; for Bunnabola is *Beanna-Beola* [Banna-Bola], the peaks of *Beola*, an old Firbolg chief, who is still remembered in tradition. See Mourne.

Tyfarnham in Westmeath; *Farannan's* house (*tigh*); the same person that gave name to Multyfarnham.

Tyone in Tipperary; *Tigh-Eóin*, John's house.

Tyrella in Down; *Tech-Riaghla* [Tee-Reela], O'C. Cal. the house of St. *Riaghal* [Reeal] or Regulus.

Tyrone. The descendants of *Eoghan* [Owen], son of Niall of the Nine Hostages, possessed the territory extending over the counties of Tyrone and Derry and the two baronies of Raphoe and Inishowen in Donegal; all this district was anciently called *Tir-Eoghain* [Tir-Owen : Wars of GG.], Owen's territory, which is now written Tyrone, and restricted to one county. See Inishowen.

Ulster; ancient Irish form *Uladh* [ulla], which with *ster* added (see Leinster), was pronounced *Ulla-ster*, and contracted to Ulster.

Ummera, Ummery, Umry; *Iomaire* [Ummera], a ridge.

Ummeracam, Umrycam; *Iomaire-cam*, crooked ridge.

Ummerafree; the ridge of the heath (*fraech*).

Unshinagh, Inshinagh; *Uinseannach*, a place producing ash trees (*uinnse* and *fuinnse*).

Uragh; *Iubhrach* [yuragh], yew land.

Urbal; a tail; from shape or position.

Urbalreagh in Antrim, Donegal, and Tyrone; grey tail.

Urbalshinny in Donegal; the fox's tail (*sionnach*), from some peculiarity of shape, or perhaps from having been a resort of foxes.

Urcher; *Urchur*, a cast or throw. See Ardnurcher.

Uregare in Limerick; *Iubhar-ghearr* [yure-yar], short yew tree.

Urney, Urny; *Urnaidhe* [Urny], an oratory. See Nurney.

Urlar, Urlaur; a floor, a level place.

Valentia Island in Kerry; so called by the Spaniards. Ancient and present Irish name, *Dairbhre* [Darrery], a place producing oaks. See Kildorrery.

Vartry river in Wicklow; a corruption of the old tribe name *Fir-tire* [Firteera], the men of the territory (*tir*).

Ventry in Kerry; got its name from a beautiful white strand, called in Irish *Fionn-traigh* [Fintra], white strand.

Wateresk; upper channel (*eisc*). See Kilwatermoy.

Waterford; a Danish name; old form Vadrefiord, the latter part of which is the northern word *fiord*, a sea inlet. Old Irish name *Port-Lairge* or Portlargy See Strangford and Carlingford.

Watergrasshill in Cork; a translation of the Irish name, *Cnocán-na-biolraighe* [Knockaun-na-billery], the little hill of the water-cresses.

Wexford; a Danish name; old form Weisford, which is said to mean west *fiord* or bay; old Irish name, *Carman.*

Wicklow; a Danish name; old forms of the name, Wkyynglo, Wygyngelo, Wykinlo. Old Irish name Kilmantan, the church of St. Mantan, one of St. Patrick's disciples. This saint, according to the Annals of Clonmacnoise and other authorities, had his front teeth knocked out by a blow of a stone, from one of the barbarians who opposed St. Patrick's landing in Wicklow; hence he was called *Mantan*, or the toothless.

Windgap, Windygap; a translation of *Bearna-na-gaeithe* [Barnanageehy], the gap of the wind.

Witter in Down; *Uachdar*, upper. See Wateresk and Eighter.

Wood of O near Tullamore in King's County; the Irish name is *Eóchaill*, yew-wood, the same as Youghal;

modern name an attempted translation :—Wood of O,
i. e. the wood of the *eó* or yew.

Yellow Batter, and Green Batter, near Drogheda; batter here means a road.   See Booterstown and Batterstown.

Yewer near Killashandra in Cavan; an anglicised form
of *Iubhar* [yure], the yew tree.   See Newry.

Youghal in Cork.   A yew wood grew anciently on the
hill slope now occupied by the town, and even yet
some of the old yews remain; hence it was called
Eochaill [Oghill], F. M., i. e. yew wood.   See Oghill
and Aughall.

VOCABULARY OF IRISH ROOT WORDS.

(The principal modern forms are given in Italica.)

——◆——

Abh [aw or ow], a river; *aw, ow.*

Abhainn [owen], a river; *owen, avon,* and in the end of words, with the *h* of the article, *hown, hone, howna, hivnia.*

Abhall [owl, ool, or avel], an apple, an apple tree; in some parts of the north it is used in the sense of "orchard." Modern forms *owl, ool, owle, aval,* &c.

Achadh [aha], a field; it is generally represented in modern names by *agha, agh,* or *augh,* but these also often stand for *ath,* a ford.

Aenach [enagh], anciently signified any assembly of the people, but it is now always applied to a cattle fair; *enagh, eeny, eena, eanig.*

Aileach [ellagh], a circular stone fort; *ellagh, elly.*

Aill [oil], a cliff; *ayle, aille,* &c. See Faill.

Aireagal [arrigal], a habitation, an oratory, a small church; *arrigle* and *errigal.*

Airne [arney], a sloe; *arney.*

Ait [aut], a place, a site; commonly made *at*: frequently combines with *teach,* a house, to form the compound *ait-tighe* [aut-tee], in modern forms *atty* or *atti,* a house site.

Aiteann [attan], furze; forms the terminations *-attin, -attina.*

Aith [ah], a kiln of any kind; made *-haia, -hagh, -haha, -hay, -hey,* and *-hoy,* in the end of names.

Alt, a height, a cliff, a glen side.

An, the Irish definite article.

Ar [awr], slaughter; *are, aur,* and *air.*

Ard, high, a height.

Ath [ah], a ford ; *ath, ah, augh, agh, a, aha, aw,* &c.

Bád [baud], a boat.

Badhun [bawn], a cow fortress, the *bawn* of a castle.

Baile [bally], a town, a townland ; *bally, balli, vally* and in the eastern counties *bal.*

Bán [bawn], white or fair coloured ; *bane, baun, bawn, vane, vaun.*

Barr [baur], the top, the highest point ; *bar, baur.* The *Bar* of a townland (used in the north) is the high or hilly part.

Beag [beg], little.

Bealach [ballagh], a road or pass ; *ballagh, vally.*

Bealltaine [beltany], the first day of May ; celebrated as a festival by the pagan Irish.

Beann [ban, ben], a horn, a gable, a peak, or pointed hill.

Beannchar [banaher], horns, gables, peaks ; *banagher, bangor.*

Bearn, bearna, bearnas [barn, barna, barnas], a gap, a gap in a mountain ; *barna, barny, varna, varny, barnis, varnis,* and often in the north *barnet.*

Bearnach [barnagh], gapped.

Beith [beh], the birch tree ; *beitheach* [behagh] a birchy place ; *behy, beha, beagh, behagh, veha, vehy,* &c.

Bél, beul [bale], the mouth, an entrance, a ford ; often joined to *ath* in the compound *bél-atha* [bellaha, bella], a ford-mouth or ford entrance.

Bile [billa], a large ancient tree ; a tree held in veneration for any reason ; *billa, billy, villa, ville, villy, bella, vella.*

Biorar [birrer], watercress ; usually corrupted to biolar [biller] ; *viller, vilra,* &c.

Bo, a cow ; *bo, boe,* and by eclipse, *moe (mbo)* ; see page 2.

Boireann [burren], a large rock, a rocky district.

Both [boh], a tent or hut ; *bo, boh, boha, bohy, voe.*

Bóthar [boher], a road ; *boher* and *voher.* In some of the eastern counties it is corrupted to *batter.* Bohereen, a little road.

Braghad [braud], the throat ; a gorge: *braid, broad, braud.*

Bran, a raven.

Breach [breagh], a wolf; occurs in the compound breachmhagh [breaghvah], wolf-field.

Bri [*bree*], a hill; *bree, bray.*

Broc [*bruck*], a badger; *brock, brick,* and, by eclipse, *mrock;* see p. 2.

Brocach [bruckagh], a badger warren; *brockagh, brocky.*

Brugh [bru], a palace, a distinguished residence; *bru, bruff.* Bruighean [breean] has the same meaning; but in modern times it is used to denote a fairy palace; *breen, bryan, breena, vreena.*

Buaile [boolia], a booley, a feeding or milking place for cows; *booley, boley, boola, voola, voula, vooly.*

Buidhe [bwee or boy], yellow; *boy, wee,* &c.

Buirghes [burris], a burgage or borough; *borris* and *burris.*

Bun, the end or bottom of anything; the mouth of a river.

Cabhan [cavan], a hollow; in some parts of Ulster it signifies a round hill; *cavan.*

Cacch [kay], blind, purblind, one-eyed; *keagh, kee.*

Caenach [keenagh], moss; *keenagh.*

Caera [*kaira*], a sheep; *keeragh,* and, eclipsed with the article, *nageeragh.*

Caerthainn [kairhan], the quicken tree; *keeran, caran, kerane, keraun.*

Cairthe [carha], a pillar stone; *carra, carha,* and *car.*

Caiseal [cashel], a circular stone fort; *cashel, castle.*

Caisleán [cushlaun], a castle; *cashlaun, cushlane.*

Cala, a marshy meadow along a river or lake; a landing place for boats; *callow* and *cala.*

Capall, a horse; *capple, cappul,* and eclipsed with the article (see p. 2), *nagappul* and *nagapple.*

Carn, a monumental heap of stones; *carn, carna.*

Carr, a rock, rocky land.

Carraig [corrig], a rock; *carrig, carrick, carriga.*

Cartron, a quarter of land (Anglo-Norman).

Casan [cassaun], a path.

Cath [cah], a battle.

Cathair [caher], a circular stone fort, a city; *caher, cahir.*

Ceallurach [calluragh], an old burial ground; *callooragh.*

Cealtrach [caltragh], an old burial ground; *caltrayk caldragh.*

Ceann [can], the head, front, or highest part of anything; *kan, can, kin, ken.*

Ceapach [cappa], a plot of ground laid down in tillage; *cappagh, cappa, cap, cappy.*

Ccard [card], an artificer; *nagard, nagarde, "of the artificers."*

Ceardcha [cardha], a forge; *carte, cart, cartan, carton.*

Ceathramhadh [carhoo], a quarter, a quarter of land, *carrow, carhoo, carrive.*

Ceide [keady], a hillock, a hill level and smooth ar top; *keady, keadew, keadagh, cady, caddagh.*

Ceis [kesh], a wicker basket, a wickerwork causeway; *kish, kesh.*

Cill [kill], a church; *kill, kil, kyle, keel, cal, kille, killa.*

Cinel [kinel], kindred, race, descendants; *kinel, kinal.*

Cladh [cly or claw], a ditch; *cly, claw, cla.*

Clann, children, a tribe; *clan, clann.*

Clar, a board, a plain; *clar, clare.*

Clais [clash], a trench; *clash.*

Cliath [clee], a hurdle.

Cloch, a stone, a stone castle; *clogh, clough, clo, clohy, cloy, naglogh.*

Clochan, a row of stepping stones across a river, sometimes a stone castle; *cloghan, cloghane, cloghaun.*

Cluain [cloon], a meadow, a fertile piece of land among bogs, marshes, or woods; *cloon, clon, clin, cloony.*

Cnap [knap], a knob, a round little hill; *knap, nap, crap, crup.*

Cnoc [knock], a hill; *knock, knick, nick, crock, cruck.*

Cobhlach [cowlagh], a fleet; *cowly, howly, coltig, holt.*

Coigeadh [coga], a fifth part, a province; *cooga, coogue*

Coill, a wood; *kil, kyle, cuill, cullia.*

Coinicer [knickere], a rabbit warren; *coneykeare, concar, conigar, conigare, kinnegar, nicker, &c.*

Coinín [cunneen], a rabbit; *coneen, nagoneen, nagoneeny.*

Coll, the hazel: *coll, col, cole, cull, cul, coyle, kyle quill.*

Congbhail [congwal], a habitation, a church; *conwal, connell, cunnagavale.*

Cor, a round hill, &c

Cora, a weir; *cor, corra, curra, cur.*

Corc, corca, race, progeny; *corku.*

Corcach, a marsh; *corcagh, corkey, cork.*

Corr, a crane or heron; *cor, gor, gore, nagor.*

Cos, a foot; *cuss, cush, cosh.*

Cot, a small boat; *cotty.*

Craebh [crave], a branch, a large branchy tree; *creeva, crew, creery, nagreeve.*

Craig [crag], a rock.

Crann, a tree; *crann, cran, crin, nagran.*

Crannog, an artificial island or lake dwelling; *crannoge, cronoge.*

Creabhar [crour], a wood-cock; *crour, nagrour.*

Creamh [crav], wild garlic.

Croch, a cross, a gallows, *crogh, crohy, crehy, creha.*

Crochaire [crohera], a hangman; *croghera, croghery, nagroghery.*

· Cros, a cross; *cross, crush, crusha.*

Cruach, cruachán [cruagh, cruhaun], a rick, a round stacked up hill; *crogh, cruagh, croagh, croghan, croaghan.*

Cruit [crit], a hump, a round little hill; *cruit, crotta, crutta, crit.*

Cu, a fierce dog, a hound—genitive *con; con, nagon, nagun.*

Cuas [coose], a cave, a cove; *coos, coose, cose, couse, goose, gose, nagoose.*

Cuil [cooil], a corner, an angle; *cool, cole.*

Cuillionn [cullion], holly; *cullion, cullen.*

Cúm [coom], a hollow, a dell or valley enclosed, except on one side, by mountains; *coom, coum, coombe.*

Currach, a marsh; *curragh, curry, curra.*

Da [daw], two; *da, daw, á.*

Daingean [dangan], a fortress: *dangan, dingin, dingle.*

Dair [dar], an oak; *dar, der, dara, darra, darragh.*

Dairbhre [darrery], an oak forest, a place producing oaks; *darrery, dorrery, darraragh, derravara.*

Daire or doire [derry], an oak grove or wood; *derry, derri, der.*

Damh [dauv], an ox; *dav, dev, daw, duff, diff, aff, uff, iff,* and by eclipse, *nanav.*

Dearc, derc [derk], a cave; *derk, dirk, dark.*

Dearg [derg], red; *derg, derrig, darrig.*

Dearmhagh [darwah], oak-plain; *durrow, durra, der. A*

Disert, a desert, a hermitage; *disert, desert, dysart, dysert, ister, ester, isert, ishart, tristle.*

Domhnach [downagh], Sunday, a church; *donagh, donna, donny, don, dun.*

Draeighean, [dreean], blackthorn; *dreen, drain, drin.*

Droichead [drohed], a bridge; *droghed, drehid, drought drait.*

Druim [drum], the back, a ridge or long hill; *drum drom, drim, drum.*

Dumha [dooa], a burial mound; *dooey, dooa, doo, doe.*

Dún [doon], a fortified fort, a kingly residence; *dun, don, doon, down.*

Dur, strong.

Each [agh], a horse; *augh, agh, eigh,* &c.

Eaglais [aglish], a church; *aglish, eglish, heagles, eglis.*

Eanach [annagh], a marsh; *annagh, anna, anny.*

Eas [ass], a waterfall; *ass, ess, assy, assa.*

Eascu, eascan [asscu, asscan], an eel; *askin.*

Edar, between; *eder, ader, adder.*

Eidhneán [īnaun], ivy; *eidneach* [inagh], an ivy-bearing place; *inane, inagh, eany, enagh.*

Eilit [ellit], a doe; *elty, ilty, elt, ilt.*

Eisc [esk], a water channel; *esk.*

Eiscir [esker], a ridge of high land, a sand hill; *esker, iskera, ascragh, eskeragh.*

En [ain], a bird; *naneane,* " of the birds."

Eó [ō], a yew tree; *o, oe, yo.*

Eochaill [oghill] a yew wood; *oghill, aughal, youghal*

Eudan [eden], the forehead, a hill brow; *eden, edn.*

Ey (Danish), an island; *ey, i, ay, eye.*

Fada, long; *fada, fad, ad, ada, adda.*

Faeileán, faeileóg [fweelaun, fweeloge], a sea gull *naweelaun, naweeloge* (" of the sea gulls"), *wheelion, eelan.*

Faill [foyle], a cliff; *foyle, foil, fall.* See Aill.

Faithche [faha], a green level space near a residence, for games, exercises, &c.; a level field; *faha, fahy fa, foy, fy, fey, feigh.*

Fásach [faussagh], a wilderness; *fasagh, fassagh, fassa.*

Feadán [faddaun], a streamlet; *faddan, feddan, fiddan, fiddane, eddan.*

Feadóg [faddoge], a plover; *viddoge, vaddoge, faddock feddock.*

Feannóg [fannoge], a scaldcrow; *finnoge, funnock, vannoge.*

Fear [far], a man; fir, feara, men; *fer, fir,* and by eclipse, *navar.*

Fearann [farran], land; *farran, farn, arran.*

Fearn, fearnóg [farn, farnoge], the alder tree; *farn, fern, farnagh, ferney, farnane, farnoge, navarn, navern, navarna.*

Fearsad [farsad], a sand bank formed in a river by the opposing currents of tide and stream; *farset, farsid, farsad, fast.*

Fert, ferta, a trench, a grave; *fert, farta, ferta, fartha, arta, navart.*

Fiach [feeagh], a raven; *ee, eha, eigh, naveagh*

Fiadh [feea], a deer; *eigh, eag, nareigh.*

Fidh [fih], a wood; *fee, fi, feigh, feth, fith, fid.*

Fionn, finn [fin], white, clear, transparent; *fin, finn, fune, foun.*

Fiord (Danish), a sea inlet; *ford.*

Fórnocht, a bare, naked, or exposed hill; *forenaght, fornaght, farnaght.*

Fraech [freugh], heath; *freagh, freugh, free, ree.*

Fuaran [fooran], a cold spring; see Uaran.

Fuinnse, fuinnseann, fuinnseóg [funsha, funshan, funshoge], the ash tree; *funcheon, funshin, funshinagh, funchoge.* The *f* is omitted in the north, giving rise to such forms as *unshin, unshinagh, inshinagh, unshog, hinchoge.*

Gabhal [goul, gole], a fork, a river fork; *goul, gole, gowel, goole, gola.*

Gabhar [gour], a goat; *gower, gour, gore.*

Gaertha [gairha], a thicket along a river; *gearha, ga ragh, geeragh, gairha, geary.*

Gall [Gaul], a foreigner, a *Gaul;* a standing stone; *gall, gal, gaul, guile, gill, gullia.*

Gallán [gallaun], a standing stone; *gallon, gullane.*

Gaeth [gwee], wind ; *gee, geeha, geehy, geeth.*

Gamhan [gowan], a calf ; *gowan, gown.*

Gamhnach [gownagh], a milch cow, a *stripper; gownagh, gawnagh.*

Garbh [garriv], rough, rugged ; *garriff, garve, garra.*

Garrán [garraun], a shrubbery ; *garran, garrane, garraun, garn.*

Gárrdha [gaura], a garden ; *garra, garry.*

Gédh [gay], a goose ; *gay.*

Glaise, glais, glas [glasha, glash, glas], a streamlet ; *glasha, glash, glas, glush.*

Glas, green ; *glass.*

Gleann [glan], a glen or valley ; *glen, glin, glynn, glan, glanna.*

Gniomh [gneeve], a measure of land ; *gneeve.*

Gobha, gen. gobhan [gow, gown], a smith ; *gow, goe, go, gown, gowan, guivna.*

Gorm, green ; *gorm.*

Gort, a tilled field ; *gort, gurt, gart.*

Greuch [greagh], a marshy place ; *greagh, greugh.*

Graig, a village ; *graigue, grag, greg.*

Grian [greean], the sun ; *green, gren, greany.*

Grianan [greenan], a summer house, a palace ; *greenan, greenane, greenaun, grenan, grennan.*

Guala [goola], the shoulder, a hill ; *goolan, golden.*

Imleach [imlagh], a marsh on the margin of a lake or river ; *emlagh, emly, imilagh.*

Inbhear [inver], the mouth of a river ; *inver, enner, ineer.*

Inis [inish], an island, a low meadow along a river ; *inis, inish, ennis, inch.*

Iolar [iller], an eagle ; *iller, uller, ilra, ulra, illard.*

Iomaire [ummera], a ridge or long hill ; *ummera, ummery, umry, amery.*

Iubhar [yure], a yew tree ; *ure.*

Ladhar [lyre, lear], a fork, a fork formed by glens or rivers ; *lyre, lear.*

Laegh [lay], a calf ; *lie, lea, leigh.*

Lag, lug ; a hollow, a hollow in a mountain ; *lag, lig, leg, lug.*

Lágh [law], a hill : *law, la.*

Lann, a house, a church; *lan, lann, land, lynn, lyn*.

Lárach [lauragh], a mare; *lara, laragh*.

Lathair. lathrach [lauher, lauragh], a site, a site of a building; *laragh, lauragh*.

Lax (Danish), a salmon; *lax, leix*.

Leaba, leabaidh [labba, labby], a bed, a grave; *labba labby*.

Leac, lic. liag [lack, lick, leeg], a flagstone; *lack, leck, lick, leek, leege*.

Leaca, Leacán [lacka, lackan], the side of a hill; *lackan, larken, lackaun, leckan, leckaun, lacka*.

Leacht [laght], a monumental heap of stones; *laght, las, let, lett*.

Leamh, leamhan [lav, lavaun], the elm tree; *levan, lerane, livaun, laune, lamph*.

Leamhchoill [lavwhill], an elm wood; *laughil, laghil, laghile, loghill, loughill, lamfield, longfield*.

Learg. leargaidh, leargan [lärg, lärgy, lärgan], the side or slope of a hill; *largy, largan*.

Leath [lah], half; *lah, la, le*.

Leathard [lahard], half height, a gentle hill; *lahard, lard*.

Léim [lame], a leap; *leam, lem, lim*.

Leithinnsi [lehinshi], half island, a peninsula; *lehinch, lakinch, lynch*.

Leitir [letter], a wet side of a hill, plural leatracha [latraha]; *letter, lattera, lettera, letteragh*.

Liagán [legaun], a pillar stone; *legan, legane, legaun leegane, leagan*.

Liath [leea], grey; *lea*.

Liathmhuine [leewinny], grey shrubbery; *leaffony, leafin, liafin, lefinn, leighmoney*.

Lios [lis], a circular earthen fort; *lis, les, lish, lass, lassa*.

Loch, a lake; *lough, low*.

Loisgreán [luskraun], corn burnt in the ear; *luskraun, loskeraun, loskeran, lustraun, lustran, lustrin*.

Loisgthe [luska]. burnt, burnt land; *lusky, losky, lusk*.

Lon, londubh [lon, londuv], a blackbird; *lun*.

Long, a ship: *long*.

Longphort [longfort], a fortress; *longford, lonart, lunkard.*

Lurga, lurgan, the shin, a long low hill; *lurraga lurgan.*

Machaire [mahera], a plain; *maghera, maghery.*

Mac-tire [macteera], a wolf; *micteera, victeera.*

Madadh, madradh [madda, maddra], a dog; *maddy, maddoo, maddra, vaddy, vaddoo, vaddra.*

Madhm [maum], an elevated mountain pass; *maum, moym.*

Mael [mwail], bald, a hornless cow, a bald or bare hill; *moyle, meel, mweel.*

Maethail [mwayhil], soft spongy land; *mohill, mothel, mothell, mehill, moyle, weehill.*

Magh [maw], a plain; *moy, ma, may, moigh, moig, muff, mo.*

Más [mauce], the thigh, a long low hill; *mace, mas, maus, mass.*

Meall [mall], a lump, a round little hill; *maul.*

Míliuc [meeluck], low marshy ground, land near a lake or river; *meelick, mellick.*

Min [meen], smooth, fine, small; *meen.*

Moin [mone], a bog; *mone, mon, mona, vone.*

Mór [more], great, large; *more, mor.*

Móta, a moat, a high mound; *moat, mota, mote.*

Mothar [moher], in the north, a cluster of trees; in the south, the ruin of a fort, or of any building; *moher.*

Muc [muck], a pig; *muck, mucky.*

Muilenn [mullen], a mill; *mullen, mullin, willin.*

Muine [money], a shrubbery; *money.*

Muintir [munter], family, people; *munter.*

Muirisc [murrisk], a sea-side marsh; *murrisk.*

Mullach [mullagh], a summit; *mullagh, mulla, mully, mul.*

Murbhach [murvah], a salt marsh along the sea; *murvagh, murvey, murragh, murreagh, murrow.*

Nás [nauce], an assembly place; *naas, nash.*

Nead [nad], a bird's nest; *nad, ned, nid, neth.*

Og [oge], young, little; *oge, og, ock.*

Oileán [oilaun], an island; *illan, illane, illaun.*

Omna, an oak; *omna, umna.*

Os, a fawn; *uss, ish.*

Piast [peeast], a beast, a worm, a serpent; *piast, peastia, beast.*

Pobul [pubble], people; *pubble, pobble, popple, pobul, phubble.*

Poll, a hole; *poll, poul, pull, pool, foyle, phuill, phull.*

Preachán [prehaun], a crow; *preaghaun.*

Puca [pooka], a *pooka* or spright; *pooka, puck, pook, phuca.*

Rath [raw], a circular fort; *rath, raw, rah, ray, ra, raha.*

Reidh [ray], a coarse mountain flat; *rea, re, rey.*

Reilig [rellig], a cemetery; *relick. relig.*

Riabhach [reeagh], grey; *reagh, rea.*

Riasc [reesk], a marsh; *riesk, reisk, risk, reask.*

Rince, rinceadh [rinka], dance; *rinky, rinka, rink.*

Rinn, a point of land; *rin, rine, reen, ring, ranna.*

Ros, generally means a wood in the south, and a peninsula in the north; *ross, rus, rush.*

Rusg, a marsh; *roosk, rusk, rusky, rusky.*

Saer [sair], a carpenter; *seer, teer.*

Sagart, a priest; *saggart, taggart, teggart.*

Saileach [saulagh], a sallow; *sillagh, sallagh, sill.*

Samhuin [sowen, savin], the first of November; *souna, sawna, hawan, haman, haven, hawna.*

Scairbh [scarriff], a shallow rugged ford; *skarriff, scarry, scarva, scarvy, scarragh.*

Scairt [scart], a thicket; *scart, scarty.*

Sceach [skagh], a whitethorn bush; *skeagh, skehy, skey, ske, skeha, skew.*

Scealp [skalp], a cleft; *scalp.*

Sceilig [skellig], a rock; *skellig.*

Sceir [sker], a sharp rock, plural sceire [skerry]; *sker skerry, skerries.*

Scrin [skreen], a shrine; *skreen, skryne, skreena.*

Seabhac [shouk], a hawk; *shoke, shock, touk, tuke.*

Sealán [shallan], a hangman's rope, a gallows; *shallon, shal'an.*

Sealg [shallog], hunting; *shallog, shellig.*

Sean [shan], old; *shan, shanna.*

Seiseadh [shesha]. a sixth part: *shesha, sheshia, sheshiv*

Seisreach [shesheragh], a measure of land; *sheshera, shesheragh, sistra.*

Seiscenn [sheskin], a marsh, a quagmire; *sheskin, seskin, teskin.*

Sidh [shee], a fairy hill, a fairy; *shee.*

Sidheán [sheeaun], a fairy hill; *sheaun, sheehaun, sheeaun, shean, sion, shane.*

Siol [sheel], seed, descendants; *shil, shel.*

Sionnach [shinnagh], a fox; *shinny, shinnagh, tinny.*

Sliabh [sleeve], a mountain; *slieve, slie, sle, lieve, lie;* and by an eclipse of *s, tleva, tlieve, tlea.*

Slighe [slee], a road or pass; *slee.*

Sluagh [sloo], a host; *sloe, tloe, tloy, tlowig.*

Snamh [snauv], swimming, a swimming ford; *snauv, snave, sna, tna, tra.*

Sradbhaile [sradvally], street-town, a town with one street; *stradbally.*

Sraid [sraud], a street; *sraud, straid, strade, strad.*

Srón [srone], the nose, a nose-like hill; *sroan, shrone, stran.*

Sruth [sruh], a stream; *sruh, srue, srough, strew.*

Sruthair [sruher], a stream; *shrule, shruel, struell, srool, sroohill.*

Sruhán [sruhaun], a stream; *sroughan, sruffaun, straffan, truan, trone.*

Ster (Danish), a place.

Stuaic [stook], a pointed pinnacle, an out jutting point of rock; *stook.*

Suidhe [see], a sitting place, a seat; *see, se, sea, shi.*

Taebh [tave], the side, a hill-side; *teeve, teev.*

Taimhleacht [tavlaght], a plague-grave, a place where those who died of a plague were interred; *tallaght, tamlaght, tamlat, tawlaght, towlaght, toulett, howlaght, hawlagh, hamlat, hamlet.*

Tamhnach [tawnagh], a green field; *tawnagh, tawny tonagh, tamnagh, tamny.*

Tarbh [tarriv], a bull; *tarriv, terriff, tarriff, tarf, tarry, herriff, harriff.*

Tate, tath; a measure of land; *tat, tate.*

Teach [tagh], a house; *tagh, ta, tee, ti, ty;* and by corruption, *sta, sti, sty.*

Teamhair [tawer], an elevated spot commanding an extensive view; *tara, touragh, tower, taur.*

Teampull [tampul], a church; *temple.*

Teine [tinna], fire; *tinny, tenny.*

Teotán [totaun], a burning or conflagration; *totaun.*

Tobar, tipra (gen. tioprad), a well; *tober, tubber, tipper, tubbrid, tibret.*

Tóchar [togher], a causeway over a bog or marsh; *togher.*

Tor, a tower, a tower-like rock; *tor.*

Torc [turk], a boar; *turk, torc, hirk, nadurk.*

Traigh [tra], a strand; *tra, traw, tray.*

Trian [treen], a third part; *treen, trean, trien.*

Triucha [truha], a cantred or district; *trough, true.*

Tromm, the elder or boor-tree; *trim, trom, trum.*

Tuaim [toom], a tumulus or burial mound; *toome, tom, toom, tum.*

Tuar [toor], a bleach green, any green field where things were put to bleach or dry; *tocr, tore, tour.*

Tulach [tulla], a little hill; *tulla, tullow, tullagh, tully, tul.*

Turlach [toorlagh], a lake that dries up in summer; *turlough, turly.*

Ua, a grandson, a descendant; plural ui or uibh [ee, iv¯] descendants; *O* (in such names as O'Brien), *hy, i, ive.*

Uagh, uaimh [ooa, ooiv], a cave, gen. uamhann [ooan]; forms the terminations *oe, oo, nahoe, nahoo, oora, ove, one, oon.*

Uaran [ooran], a cold spring; *oran.*

Ubhall [ool], an apple; see abhall.

Uisce [iska], water; *iska, isky, isk.*

Urchur [urker], a cast or throw; *urcher.*

Urnaidhe [urny], a prayer, a prayer-house or oratory, *urney,* and with the article incorporated, *nurny.*

THE END.